U.S. NATIONAL PARKS TRAVEL GUIDE

DISCOVER SOME OF AMERICA'S LONELIEST TREASURES AND SURROUNDING AREAS

A World of Wander Travel Guide

by Beatrix & Zia

TABLE OF CONTENTS

INTRODUCTION

In every walk with nature, one receives far more than he seeks. -John Muir

Hello! We're Beatrix and Zia, two lifelong travel companions. We have created this travel guide just for YOU.

Are you ready to start a new adventure or open a new life chapter? Maybe this is something you have been thinking about for years or even an "Aha" moment. You might feel bored or unmotivated as your house suddenly seems too empty or quiet. We know what that's like.

Your children have "left the nest", and perhaps now you are looking to get out and do some exploring. What an exciting time! Whether you and your partner are looking forward to trying out some new activities and spending more quality time together, or you and a friend or two have been dying to try out some long-term bucket list trips together, we hope this book is just what you need to be able to get out there and indulge in some of America's most stunning and interesting landscapes while developing exciting interests and discovering new hobbies along the way.

If you recognize yourself in the above lines, you're no different from most parents and empty-nesters who look for new adventures. At a certain moment in life, our children decide that it's time for them to leave their parents' house and become independent. They move in with their partners, go on their own adventures, or go off to college. You might feel a little lost, or you might actually feel like you are reborn and about to embark on an exciting and liberating time in your life. You are ready to start this newest chapter and couldn't be more excited—maybe even a little nervous. There are likely a lot of mixed emotions happening. I know for us there were. Change can be difficult for most people, no matter how positive, and this is certainly a big life change! You might be looking forward to reconnecting with those you did not have as much time for before. You might also be thrilled to learn new things about yourself, your partner, and your friends, all while exploring brave new destinations. In both cases, you might decide to start your own adventure. Therefore, you might look for ways to enjoy this brand-new life chapter. If you're a nature lover, you might think visiting national parks is a good way to enjoy your newfound freedom, and we would agree with you.

You may however struggle to find the information you need based on what you want and look for in a national park. Before choosing this book, you might have tried different routes to find the information you were seeking, but with no luck. You might not be looking for more popular places where you know you'll always find crowds, chaos, traffic, noise, and long lines. You feel like visiting national parks because you enjoy spending time in nature, walking, and immersing yourself in the amazing landscapes, wildlife, scenic drives, and any number of other activities they offer. You might look for places where you can turn off your phone and just enjoy the sights and sounds. Everyone knows about places like Yosemite and the Grand Canyon, and while they are of course incredible, you won't necessarily find the same peace and serenity that the parks featured in this book offer! You look for spots that are off the beaten path, but totally worth the effort. However, you might not be an expert and feel like you need some guidance to choose the perfect national park for you. Until now, you might have tried reading online articles, blogs, forums, and books, and searching for all the information that was available to you. You want to be well-prepared and informed for this adventurous excursion (and that is smart!). You might feel overwhelmed by all the tips, facts, and advice you found and wonder if they're truly helpful.

Thanks to this book, you'll finally find all that you're looking for and more! Escape the madness of crowded tourist destinations and embrace the magic of the "lesser-known" national parks. *U.S. National Parks Travel Guide* is a thoughtfully curated guide that caters to the desires of all the empty-nesters out there, offering a range of enjoyable activities that go beyond rugged hikes. From scenic drives to picturesque picnic spots and leisurely walks, you can savor the beauty of nature at your own pace. Uncover hidden gems, relish tranquil moments, and create cherished memories; all in the embrace of untouched landscapes that promise an enriching and stress-free travel experience. As you'll discover, this book is designed to make it easy for you to visit these miraculous and breathtaking locations.

In the next seven chapters, we'll discuss seven national parks that might not receive the same level of attention as their more famous counterparts but are no less spectacular in their offerings. Chapter 1 will focus on the Badlands National Park, Chapter 2 on Shenandoah National Park, and Chapter 3 on Capitol Reef. Chapter 4 will discuss Voyageurs National Park, Chapter 5, North Cascades, Chapter 6, Guadalupe Mountains, and Chapter 7, Great Basin. In the conclusion, you'll find two hidden gems that we highly recommend, in case seven national parks are not enough to satisfy your curiosity and desire to travel. In each chapter, you'll find all the information you need to prepare yourself to visit the respective national park, from basic information to different hiking trails you can try. Don't feel disheartened if you're not an expert hiker—there will be something for all tastes. In addition, you'll also find useful information about surrounding areas where you can visit amazing cities, try restaurants, or simply sleep at night. For each park, you'll find everything you need to know, from the most practical tips to some fun facts and trivia. At the end of each chapter, you'll also find a blank page that you can use as you please to jot down ideas, dreams, plans, and whatever crosses your mind.

Here are some fun facts about national parks.

- President Woodrow Wilson officially established the National Park Service (NPS) on August 25th, 1916 (Dierickx, 2015).

- The NPS is responsible for the conservation of wildlife, natural and historic objects, and scenery. It must also take care of nature to give everyone—even future generations—the opportunity to enjoy it. Therefore, the NPS must make sure national parks aren't damaged or neglected. Now, the NPS is more than 100 years old and busier than ever. In fact, they keep protecting more than 400 sites, including national monuments, battlefields, seashores, and much more. In total, the NPS protects more than 84 million acres of nature.

- Which was the very first ever U.S. national park? It's Yellowstone, which was founded in 1872 (Dierickx, 2015).

- National parks offer much more than just historical fun facts, as they also provide many benefits to our physical and mental health.

- Research has found that spending just 20 minutes in nature can improve your concentration, impulse control, problem-solving, critical thinking, and even relationship skills (Seely, 2021).

- Time in nature helps you create a deep connection with it, your inner self, and your loved ones. Consequently, it also allows you to develop your spirituality.

- An easy hike in a national park can already be enough to make you reflect on yourself, your values, and your beliefs.

- Research has also discovered that spending time in nature increases our generosity and cooperative behaviors, and reduces symptoms of stress, anxiety, and depression. National parks can improve your overall well-being (Seely, 2021).

- Visiting national parks allows you to move naturally and enjoy nature and life's simple pleasures.

- Exploring new places also improves cognitive function, as trying new activities creates new connections in your brain and helps you keep it healthy and active.

Thanks to our passion for traveling and exploring new places, we've been fortunate enough to visit each of the National Parks featured in this book. We're also empty-nesters and are having the time of our lives! After our children went off on their own and became independent, we realized it was time for our next life chapter to begin and we were all for it. We knew the world was waiting for us. Since we started this new journey, we've been discovering new interests, places, hobbies, foods, cultures, and people. We believe the world is our oyster and we intend to partake. After our children started living their own lives, we packed our bags and followed our dream of visiting some of the less-traveled and loneliest national parks and the hidden gems that surround them. Obviously, we made some mistakes, didn't always have all the necessary information, and had some troubles along the way. This is why we decided to craft this guide—you deserve to enjoy these places hassle-free. Learn from our mistakes!

This is just the first book in a series. We're thrilled and grateful to be able to create such a useful bundle of books chronicling some of our most beloved travels and adventures as brand-new empty-nesters. Spurred by our newfound free time and a very long bucket list of places to experience, we wanted to create a book of travel destinations that are meaningful, awe-inspiring, and fun while also lacking in the chaos that many times accompanies travel, especially to many national parks. U.S. National Parks Travel Guide comprises some of the most scenic, historic, and picturesque landscapes and activities known to man. The parks and surrounding places of note highlighted in this book are no less magnificent or glorious than some of the more popular national parks, just a little more off the beaten path but so well worth the effort.

Thanks to this book, you'll identify those geographic treasures that have not been spoiled by the masses. If you are someone who is looking for the special grandeur provided by the less traveled national parks, yet do not know where to even begin to gather the information, this is your one-stop shop! We have gathered for you a variety of options related to lodging, transportation, dining, groceries, scenic drives, hikes, and much more! We have even included our favorite surrounding locations, some of which are even more special than the national parks themselves, in our humble opinion! Through the experiences and information this book will offer you, you will discover new hobbies and interests, like canoeing, birding, nature photography, hiking, fishing, and the RV lifestyle.

This book is a complete guide for everything you need to know to explore and enjoy these special and "lonely" lesser-known U.S. treasures. At our age, we love having a tangible book where we can look information up, underline things, take notes, and have them available to us regardless of cell service.

Get an Annual National Park Pass and let's go!

CHAPTER ONE: BADLANDS NATIONAL PARK & SURROUNDING TREASURES, SOUTH DAKOTA

If you truly love nature, you will find beauty everywhere. -Laura Ingalls Wilder

The Badlands National Park in South Dakota is the first national park we'll discuss in this book. Established in 1978, it comprises more than 240,000 acres and is characterized by unique landscapes, like towering spires, breathtaking rock formations, and steep canyons (Mecelin, 2022). The Badlands National Park was also home to Native Americans for generations. Did you know that it was merely a shallow sea millions of years ago? Over the millennia, sediments of silt, clay, and sand accumulated, creating the rock formations you can see today. The uncommon shapes and colored stripes were created by the water that covered the area. However, the process of transformation didn't end millennia ago. Even today, you can witness the effects of erosion that keeps changing the natural landscapes. Don't worry, it won't disappear if you don't plan to visit it soon, as the erosion advances only one inch per year (Mecelin, 2022).

You might wonder why this national park is so special. Well, you'll see colorful rock formations you won't be able to see anywhere else in the world. You'll also have the opportunity to spot bison, blooming cactus, wildflowers, and much more. What we, Beatrix and Zia, loved most about this park, other than its magical and "otherworldly" appearance, were the breathtaking sunrises and sunsets. Whether you are someone who likes to get up early and enjoy the sunrise with a cup of coffee, like Zia, or a person who prefers a glass of wine and a picnic during sunset, like Beatrix, you will not be disappointed. Another thing we greatly appreciated about this park is that you do not have to trek for miles on difficult hikes to experience the best views. Most panoramas could be reached via short paved or board walks or easy-to-navigate hiking trails. The Badlands offers the perfect mix of exercise and jaw-dropping landscapes. You cannot beat that combo! From the free-roaming bison to the blooming cactus to the rainbow rock formations, you will be in awe and so grateful you made the journey.

Basic Information

Location

25216 Ben Reifel Road, Interior SD 57750.

Entrance Passes

To enjoy the amenities of the park, you must pay a fee. If you want, you have the opportunity to buy the annual entrance at $55.00. With that, you can access the park whenever you want over a period of one year, starting from the moment you buy the pass. Otherwise, you'll have to pay between $15.00 and $30.00 depending on how you decide to visit the park—whether you just need a ticket to take a walk inside, or you have a motorcycle or a private vehicle. You'll have to pay the same fee all year round (Basic Information- Badlands National Park, 2021).

Interagency Passes

If you want to visit more than one national park, you might consider getting one of the interagency passes issued by the National Park Service (Entrance Passes, 2019). You can buy them online from the USGS Online Store, at national parks, or other federal recreation sites. If you buy your pass online, make sure to order it in advance, as it might take more than three weeks to process the order and deliver your pass.

- **The Annual Pass:** It costs $80.00 and is available to everyone between the ages of 16 and 62.

- **The Military Annual Pass:** It's completely free and available for U.S. military members and their dependents in all military forces, like the Navy, Army, Space, and Marines.

- **The Military Lifetime Pass:** It's also free but available only for Gold Star Families and U.S. veterans.

- **The 4th Grade Pass:** It's available for all students attending the 4th grade of school or home-schooled and aged 10. The pass is free from the beginning of the 4th grade school year until September of the following year.

- **The Senior Pass:** If you're 62 or over, you can get a Senior Pass. You can choose between the Annual Pass, which costs $20.00, and the Lifetime Pass, which is $80.00. The Senior Pass provides a 50% discount on some fees charged for facilities and services, like swimming or camping.

- **The Access Pass:** It's specifically designed for all U.S. citizens with permanent disabilities. It's completely free and valid for life. Like the Senior Pass, the Access Pass can provide a 50% discount on some amenity fees.

- **The Volunteer Pass:** It's a free annual pass you can get by volunteering for more than 250 hours for a federal agency that participates in the program of Interagency Pass (Entrance Passes, 2019).

Which pass best suits your needs? Go online or to one of the federal recreation sites and get your interagency pass.

Operating Hours and Seasons

Badlands National Park is open all day, every day, all year round (Operating Hours & Seasons - Badlands National Park, 2020). However, make sure to check road conditions before leaving for your trip in winter. Some roads might be icy or even closed.

Inside the park, you'll find two visitor centers: Ben Reifel, at park headquarters, and White River, at the Pine Ridge Reservation. In both visitor centers you'll find rangers who can answer all your questions about the national park, distribute maps and other useful material, and provide directions. You will also find exhibits and restroom facilities. Ben Reifel is open all year round while White River is open only during the summer season, from May to September. For more information about Ben Reifel, you can call (605) 433-5361. For more information about White River, you can call (605) 455-2878 (Operating Hours & Seasons - Badlands National Park, 2020).

Best Times to Visit

At this point, you might wonder when's the best time to visit Badlands National Park. We would suggest you go there during spring when temperatures are moderate—around 81 °F—and there aren't many crowds. Between April and June, lodging and transportation options are likely to be more reasonably priced as well. In addition, you'll be surprised by the diverse wildflowers you'll see during that season. If we were you, we would absolutely avoid visiting Badlands National Park during summer, especially July and August. Those are the busiest months and temperatures are extremely high, reaching up to 116 °F. At night, they can drop as low as 40 °F (Longe, 2022).

If you can't go during spring, you can also give it a try during fall, especially between the end of September and beginning of October. At that time, you won't find many visitors and temperatures will be around the 80 °F range as in spring. If you enjoy the cold and prefer traveling during winter, we suggest you visit the park between December and January. As you might guess, you won't find any crowds and the Ben Reifel visitor center will be all for you. You can also enjoy an amazing hike or a snowshoeing experience. The breathtaking landscapes become even more magical and mystical at this time of the year. Just make sure to prepare yourself for the cold, as temperatures can drop as low as 11 °F (Longe, 2022). Always check the weather forecast before heading to the park.

In general, spring and fall are the best times of the year to visit Badlands National Park, so choose the season that speaks to you most.

How to Get There

You can get to Badlands National Park by car or plane.

Car

- **Interstate 90:** If you go by car, you'll probably cross the Interstate 90, which is the most popular route to reach the park. Moreover, it provides easy access to the spectacular Badlands Loop Road. From Rapid City, you have to drive east for more or less 60 miles until you reach a small town called Wall. From there, you can reach the Pinnacles Entrance of Badlands. Interstate 90 is a major highway open all year round also accessible to RVs, as it is mostly flat.

- **Highway 44:** From Rapid City, you can enter Highway 44 and keep driving until you reach the Interior Entrance of the park. This road is less trafficked than the Interstate 90 and directly connects you with the South Unit of the park, which is less popular than the main entrance. Highway 44 is flat, like Interstate 90, so it's suitable for RVs, and still leads you to the Badlands Loop Road.

- **Highway 240:** When you look at maps, you might find another highway called Highway 240, which is just another name for the Badlands Loop Road. It's 39-miles long and gives you the opportunity to stop and admire the view at more than 12 scenic overlooks from the comfortable seat of your vehicle. Highway 240 might be curvy at times, but it's still RV-friendly.

Plane

- **Rapid City Regional Airport:** It's the closest airport and is about an hour away from the Pinnacle Entrance of Badlands. It's open all year but only receives flights from a few major U.S. cities, such as Chicago, Las Vegas, Dallas, Denver, and Phoenix. If you fly from anywhere else, you'll probably need to stop at one of the above cities before reaching the Rapid City Regional Airport.

- **Casper International Airport:** It's the closest international airport and is about five hours distant from the park, but it doesn't provide many flights. In most cases, you'll probably have to lay over in Salt Lake City or Denver.

- **Denver International Airport:** It has many flight options and you might find cheaper tickets. However, it takes almost seven hours to reach Badlands National Park. If you want, you can take a flight to Denver and then to the Rapid City Regional Airport to get a bit closer.

- **Billings-Logan International Airport:** It's about six hours away from Badlands and has more flight options than Casper.

Transportation & Car Rentals in South Dakota

If you decide to arrive by plane, you might want to rent a car. You'll find a list of car rentals close to the park below.

- **Black Hills Car Rentals:** It provides a range of vehicles from cars to pickup trucks and vans. If you come from the airport, they also offer free pick up and drop off. For more information, you can call (605) 342-6696.

- **Casey's Auto Rental:** You might be interested in renting a vehicle at Casey's Auto Rental if you want to rent a van or SUV. They also offer free pick up within 10 miles of their location. For more information, you can call (605) 343-2277 or (866) 748-2277.

- **Shebby Lee Tours:** This company offers tours all around the West—even the Old West! You can choose between taking a walk or a jeep ride in the wide-open spaces of the area. For more information, you can call (605) 390-0211.

- **Jack's Campers:** If you're looking for an RV, you can rent one at Jack's Campers. In South Dakota, there are two branches and the closest one to the park is in Piedmont. For more information, you can call (605) 787-9010 or (877) 356-1812.

- **Cruise America:** If you want to rent an RV, you can visit the website www.cruiseamerica.com. It allows you to rent the RV you want anywhere in the USA! In South Dakota, you can find RV rentals at Black Hills Auto Grooming. To reserve a rental, you can call (800) 671-7839. If you just want some more information, you can call (605) 791-5432.

- **Turo:** If you don't want to spend a lot of money on renting, you can also rent a car through the Turo app from a local resident! It's much more affordable in many cases. If you want to try this experience, you just need to download the app, choose your destination, and find the ride of your choice. It's the method we, Beatrix and Zia, prefer when a car rental is in order.

Accommodations

Now that you know how to reach Badlands National Park, you can look for places to stay.

- **Whispering Pines Bed & Breakfast Outfitters:** It's just six miles south of the main entrance of the park and offers guided hunts, an RV park, and also a 2,700 square-foot hunting lodge. RV sites are equipped with sewer, water, and electrical hook-ups, so you'll find yourself at ease there. Alternatively, you can book one of the eight cabins with large rooms. For more information, you can call (605) 433-5490.

- **Econo Lodge:** Econo Lodge Hotels are easy to book and not too expensive, so you can give them a try. In particular, we suggest you go to the hotel in Wall, which is one of the closest cities to the Badlands National Park. The hotel is also pet-friendly. For more information, you can call (605) 279-2121.

- **Badlands Hotel & Campground:** The main advantage of this accommodation is that you'll only be one mile away from the park, so you'll be able to get there by walking. Moreover, you can choose between staying in a hotel or a full-service campground. Badlands Hotel & Campground also offers an onsite restaurant. For more information, you can call (605) 433-5335.

- **Cedar Pass Lodge:** Cedar Pass Lodge welcomes guests to enjoy the incredible beauty of the park, as the only in-park accommodation. It also offers cabins and the possibility to camp. It provides a restaurant where you can get breakfast, lunch, and dinner. The RV park and campgrounds are open between April and October. Before deciding to sleep here, make sure to check the website to see when they're open. For more information, you can call (855) 765-0737. You can also complete the available form on their website to send them specific questions or doubts.

- **Best Western Plains Motel:** In addition to the Econo Lodge, you can also find the Best Western Plains Motel in Wall, which has all the features a person needs and is pet-friendly. For more information, you can call 1(800) 780-7234.

- **Circle View Guest Ranch:** The ranch is situated on Highway 44, just an hour away from Rapid City, thus its location is perfect to easily reach Badlands National Park. What distinguishes this ranch from all other options is that it's been family owned and operated for more than 15 years and has an original 1880 Homestead Cabin. For more information, you can call (605) 433-5582.

- **Koa Holiday:** It's located in Rapid City and easy to access. It's perfect if you travel with a camper and look for a cozy camping cabin, if you have an RV, or if you just want to sleep in a tent. For more information, you can call (605) 348-2111.

- **Lake Park Campground & Cottages:** It's located close to Rapid City and provides RV and tent campground, cottages, or tiny cozy homes to relax during your stay at Badlands. To reserve a spot, you can call (605) 341-5320.

- **Airbnb:** I'm sure you've heard about it! In this app, you can find all sorts of accommodation: Apartments, guesthouses, cottages, bungalows, and much more. This is a great way to learn about the area from the locals while supporting them as well.

- **VRBO:** If you don't find what you're looking for on Airbnb, you can also look at Vrbo, which is a valid alternative. In fact, you can find an infinite number and type of accommodations in this app.

Restaurants

Looking for a place to eat during your stay at Badlands National Park? Try out the following recommended places.

- **Wagon Wheel Bar & Grill:** This is not a proper restaurant, but still worth it. It's a bar that also serves food. Its address is 115 Main Street, Interior 57750. For more information, you can call (605) 433-5331.

- **Wall Drug Store, INC:** Since 1931, Wall Drug has transformed from a humble place to get something to eat into an oasis for all tourists (Welcome to Wall Drug, n.d.). You won't only find food there, but also gifts, souvenirs, plenty of activities to try, and all the information you need to properly visit Badlands. This place is a must visit! The address of the restaurant is 510 Main Street, Wall, 57790-0401. For more information, you can call (605) 279-2175.

- **Cedar Pass Lodge & Restaurant:** As already mentioned previously, Cedar Pass Lodge also provides a restaurant for visitors. We suggest you try their Famous Indian Tacos, with their own fresh fry bread, seasoned beef and buffalo meat. They also offer a vegetarian version of this famous taco! The highlight of this restaurant is the location, as you can comfortably sit and enjoy your meal while gazing at the breathtaking Badlands.

- **Cowboy Corner:** Cowboy Corner is the perfect spot if you want to eat something fast while also filling the tank. It provides a gas station and serves lunch from Monday to Thursday and dinner from Friday to Sunday. The address of the restaurant is 500 SD Highway 377, Interior 57750. For more information, you can call (605) 433-5333.

Shops, Groceries, or Markets Nearby

What if you want to buy a souvenir, gift, or something to remember the amazing time you spent in Badlands? You can choose among the best street markets of the area listed below.

- **Cedar Pass Lodge:** At Cedar Pass Lodge you can sleep, eat, and also buy a souvenir. The gift shop will surely surprise you for its unique items.

- **Badlands Trading Post:** Badlands Trading Post is a one-of-a-kind place where you can fill the tank and buy original articles like western artwork and personalized clothes. The address is 21290 SD-240, Philip.

- **Wall Drug Store:** As you already learned, Wall Drug Store is more than just a restaurant! Go see it for yourself. Check the previous section for contact information.

- **Panorama Point:** If you want to stop and enjoy the panorama between lunch break and shopping, you can go to Panorama Point, which offers stunning views over the Badlands. You can easily access Panorama Point from the city of Wall.

- **Badlands Ranch Store:** If you want to meet some wild animals, this is the place. The store allows you to buy snacks to give to the prairie dogs of the area. Just get them and go outside—prairie dogs will naturally come to you! You can also find fascinating souvenirs from the 1950s and supplies for all tourists and hikers. The address is 21190 SD-240, Philip.

- **Dakota Sky Stone:** We highly recommend you visit Dakota Sky Stone for various reasons, one of them being the owner's kindness and friendliness. The store mainly sells turquoise jewelry and the owner is always available to help you choose the right piece. The address is 511 Main St, Wall.

- **Golddiggers:** If you're looking for a unique jewelry store, Golddiggers is the right place for you. There, you can find all sorts of accessories for men and women, from necklaces to earrings, and much more. The address is 505 Main St, Wall.

- **Badlands Harley Davidson:** This store doesn't need much explanation. If you're a fan of motorcycles and love the brand Harley Davidson, then you must stop by! The address is 601 Main St, Wall.

- **Wall Food Center:** Despite its name, the Wall Food Center is a small grocery store, but it has everything you need. Prices are reasonable and you can find plenty of supplies and items you might need. Employees are also friendly and fast at serving you. The address is 103 South Blvd, Wall.

Gas Stations

Now, let's look at all the places where you can fill the tank close to Badlands National Park.

- **Cowboy Corner:** Located at 500 Sd Hwy 377 Interior.

- **Badlands Trading Post:** Located at 21290 Sd Hwy 240, Philip.

- **Kadoka Gas & Go:** Located at 501 Sd Hwy 73, Kadoka.

- **Phillips 66:** Located at 805-899 Glenn St, Wall.

- **Yesway:** Located at 24475 S Creek Road, Kadoka 57543 and it's open 24/7.

- **Common Cents Food Store:** Located at 207 S Blvd, Wall 57790 and it's open 24/7.

- **Coyles Standard Service:** Located at 85 E US Highway 14, Philip.

Breweries and Wineries

If you're like Beatrix, you might enjoy taking a glass of wine while gazing at stunning scenery. That's why we've also included a section about breweries and wineries, which there is no shortage of! After a day of hiking and exploring the parks, we love to reward ourselves further with a hearty local beer or a flavorful wine. In fact, you can choose among a variety of places where you can get excellent beer or wine—many times locally crafted! Take some rest and enjoy the sun going down after a long exciting day. They're also all pet-friendly—in case you have decided to bring your fur friend with you.

- **Crow Peak Brewing Company:** Located at 125 Highway 14, Spearfish.

- **Spearfish Brewing Company:** Located at 741 North Main Street, Spearfish.

- **Belle Joli' Winery Sparkling House:** Located at 3951 Vanocker Canyon Road, Sturgis.

- **Sturgis Brewing Company:** Located at 600 Anna Street, Sturgis.

- **Jacobs Brewhouse & Grocer:** Located at 79 Sherman Street, Deadwood.

- **Naked Winery Tasting Room & Sick-N-Twisted Brew Pub:** Located at 692 Upper Main Street, Deadwood.

- **Cohort Craft Brewery:** Located at 4905 5th Street, Rapid City.

- **Dakota Shivers Brewing:** Located at 717 West Main Street, Lead.

- **Lost Cabin Beer Company:** Located at 1401 West Omaha Street, Rapid City.

All of the above breweries and wineries are unique! Just choose the one (or ones!) that sound like the best fit for your preferences.

Rules and Regulations

Badlands National Park might be more dangerous than you think, so don't underestimate the instability of the terrain. Choose the right clothes and gear before going and take all possible precautions. When you're in your vehicle, always observe speed limits and drive slowly when you spot wild animals alongside or on the road. You can camp in the park overnight but campfires aren't allowed. While walking inside the park, you can't remove any fossils, rocks or artifacts that you might find. Always respect the place and preserve the environment. If you want to visit the park by bike, you're only allowed on designated roads and you can't cross park trails. If you have a pet, you can't enter public buildings or cross trails. As mentioned above, much of this area is closed in winter so be sure to check before embarking on this journey! Pets are only allowed on paved or gravel roads and must always be kept on a leash.

For a full list of any park rules and regulations be sure to visit www. allblackhills.com.

History and Trivia

Let's learn something more about Badlands National Park! In 1939, it was established as a national monument and became a park only in 1978, as mentioned in the introduction (Pattiz, 2023c). For thousands of years, the park was used by Native Americans for their hunting grounds. The descendants of the first known hunters still live in the area and are called the Three Affiliated Tribes (Pattiz, 2023c).

Nowadays, the park is home to some of the most endangered species in all the USA (Pattiz, 2023c). These include the American bison, the bighorn sheep, the prairie dog, and the black footed ferret.

A fun fact about the park: It has played a cameo role in some famous Hollywood movies (Pattiz, 2023c). For example, it appears in Armageddon, Dust of War, and Starship Troopers. A cult movie completely set in Badlands National Park that you've probably heard about (if not watched more than once!) is Dances With Wolves.

Scenic Drives and Overlooks

Badlands National Park is one of the most accessible national parks of the USA, as you can easily visit it by car (Bram, 2023). You can enjoy the most scenic overlooks comfortably sitting in your vehicle. In fact, all the panoramas you'll discover next can be easily viewed from the Badlands Loop Road or Highway 240.

- **Big Badlands Overlook:** It's one of the most sensational overlooks of the park. We recommend you go there to watch the sunrise.

- **Ancient Hunters Overlook:** It has archaeological significance, as most evidence of ancient human activity was found here.

- **Prairie Wind Overlook:** It doesn't offer any views of the Badlands but provides an exclusive glimpse of the prairie.

- **White River Valley Overlook:** This is the perfect spot for taking pictures, especially at sunset.

- **Burns Basin Overlook:** It's a great place to spot prairie dogs.

- **Bigfoot Pass Overlook:** In addition to the stunning views, this place also has historical significance. It derives its name from Big Foot, chief of the Native American tribe called Miniconjou Lakota. He used this pass to escape the U.S. Army before being captured (Bram, 2023).

- **Conata Basin Overlook:** Here, you can see all the geological layers of the park. You must absolutely go!

- **Yellow Mounds Overlook:** This place provides a spectacular sight of the rock layers that characterize the area.

- **Homestead Overlook:** It offers an amazing view of both the prairie and the Badlands.

- **Pinnacles Overlook:** This is the most popular overlook because it's the highest point in the park that provides a 180-degree vista. You must try this unique experience.

Things to Do in the Park

There is no shortage of unique and interesting activities in the park. In the previous sections, you discovered all the amazing scenery you can view from the Badlands Loop Road. Crossing that route is spectacular and you should absolutely do it! But there's much more you can do in the park, as you'll find out next.

- **Visit the Fossil Preparation Lab:** You have the opportunity to learn more about ongoing science in the park and watch paleontologists at work!

- **Enjoy the night sky:** Whenever you decide to visit the park, you'll always have the chance to contemplate more than 7,500 stars (Enjoy the Night Sky, 2021). In particular, you can see the Milky Way Galaxy with unexpected clarity.

- **Spotting wildlife:** Among all the wild animals you can find in the park, the most fascinating ones you can spot are the bison, bighorn sheep, and prairie dog.

- **Drive around the South Unit:** This route is an alternative to the famous Badlands Loop Road and provides spectacular sights.

- **Drive Sage Creek Rim Road:** Along the way, you can stop at some lesser-known overlooks that will amaze you.

- **Badlands sunrises and sunsets:** Wherever you go inside the park, you'll always be in the right spot to enjoy the sunrise or sunset. Just choose an overlook and observe the sky.

- **Hiking Badlands back roads with your dog:** We recommend you go to the Old Northeast Road to enjoy a relaxed walk with your pet.

- **Horseback riding:** Day rides and horse rental aren't available, but you can still visit the park on the back of a horse.

Did this list spark your curiosity? If you want to know more, you can visit the website of the National Park Service or go to the visitor center once you arrive at the park.

Hiking Trails

One of the things you must do if you visit Badlands National Park is hiking, obviously You'll find a list of the most fascinating hikes, from the easiest to the most strenuous trail, below. They're all round trips.

- **Fossil Exhibit Trail:** It's a fully accessible, easy hike of 0.25 miles.

- **Window Trail:** It's also easy and 0.25 miles long.

- **Medicine Root Loop:** It's a rolling trail of 4 miles that is a bit more strenuous than the previous two.

- **Cliff Shelf:** It's 0.5 miles long and a moderate hike. If you plan to go there, get ready to climb stairs and pass along boardwalks.

- **Castle Trail:** It's a 10-mile, moderate hike. It's the longest trail in the park.

- **Notch Trail:** It's a short hike (just 1.5 miles) but considered moderate to strenuous. It's dangerous, especially during or after heavy rains and we don't recommend you try it if you're afraid of heights.

- **Saddle Pass:** It's a strenuous 0.25-mile trail. It's not recommended if you're not an expert hiker.

If you want to know more about each trail, you can use the AllTrails app, which gives you all the necessary details of the hike, like level of difficulty, elevation, access, photos, and reviews. AllTrails is a must have app for hikers.

When hiking, always take plenty of water and be sure to wear the proper footwear and clothing. Hiking boots or shoes should always fit snuggly to prevent blistering. Hiking boots with ankle support is ideal. Be sure your clothing is non-restrictive, comfortable and appropriate for the temperature and weather. Hiking sticks are a great consideration, especially if the trail you'll be hiking is rocky or uneven, or if the hike involves a lot of elevation gain. Beatrix especially enjoys hiking sticks when crossing rivers or creeks and rock hopping is involved. Definitely prevents spills!

Surrounding Treasures

Badlands National Park is absolutely worth it and you must visit it, but there's still much more you can do outside the park. In fact, the area is surrounded by treasures you must see at least once in your life.

- **Mount Rushmore:** Surrounded by the Black Hills National Forest, it's an extraordinary sight. In addition to the legendary colossal sculpture, you can also visit the Sculptor's Studio to learn more about the area.

- **Black Hills National Forest:** It occupies part of South Dakota and Wyoming and it's 65 miles wide (Nearby Attractions, n.d.). Here, you can find the highest point east of the renowned Rockies. The forest truly looks like a magical place where you can lose yourself. You'll find relaxing streams and lakes, bold canyons, and open grassland parks.

- **Wind Cave National Park:** It's a 28,000-acre natural sanctuary with one of the longest caves in the world. It is so incredible to tour these caves. Truly remarkable and an unforgettable experience!

- **Jewel Cave National Monument:** It's the third longest cave in the world, being 120 miles long (Nearby Attractions, n.d.).

- **Crazy Horse Memorial:** It's a work-in-progress, magnificent sculpture. Works began in 1948 and are still ongoing (Nearby Attractions, n.d.).

- **The Mammoth Site in Hot Springs:** It's a renowned fossil excavation site where kids have the chance to excavate.

- **Yellowstone National Park:** There's not much to say about it except that it's a must-go for everyone. Unique geysers, hot springs, rolling hills, and a great variety of wildlife characterize the park. As mentioned in the introduction, this is the first ever national park in the USA, and also the first in the world!

- **Personal Note from Beatrix & Zia:** Custer State Park is our absolute favorite state park! It should be a national park as far as we are concerned. The donkeys here are a personal favorite of Beatrix (petting the wild donkeys on the roadside) whereas Zia loves driving through the Needles Eye Tunnel, and watching the rock climbers. Our favorite hike there is the Sylvan Lake Shore Trail, an easy hike where you can enjoy the rock and lake views the entire way around—absolutely remarkable and a must-do. You can thank us later. The scenic drives here are some of the best anywhere if truly mind-blowing scenic drives are your thing. If you only have time for one, we highly recommend Needles Highway. This park is chock-full of paved cycling trails, too! Bring your bikes. It is a perfect way to enjoy and experience the park! It is definitely a favorite.

Nearby Cities

Don't stop at the surrounding treasures but take a walk in one of the nearby cities that might surprise you in one way or another.

- **Rapid City:** Nestled in the heart of the Black Hills, it's a must-go for all tourists who visit the area. Rapid City provides numerous attractions and parks suited for everyone. If you want, you can just take a walk around the city and enjoy a mix of art and culture, like the many murals and street art, or the bronze replicas of former U.S. Presidents. In particular, we suggest you visit the downtown area, where local culture, entertainment, dining, and history blend.

- **Central Hills Region:** From here, you can visit Mount Rushmore and the Crazy Horse Memorial. Among the cities of the area, we recommend Hill City, a picturesque small town, and Keystone, perfect if you're looking for outdoor adventures.

- **Northern Hills Region:** If you're passionate about stories of the Wild West and the gold rush days, this is the place! There, you can visit the haunts of the notorious Calamity Jane and other legendary figures.

- **Southern Hills Region:** Here, you can find loads of attractions, from the famous Rocky Mountains to the Wind Cave National Park and Custer Park.

- **Black Hills of Wyoming Region:** This is the part of the Black Hills National Forest that crosses the border with Wyoming. In Newcastle, you can explore historic buildings, while in Hulett, you can savor the local cowboy culture and the state's best burgers.

- **Lakota:** In the area of Badlands, Native American tribes lived and hunted for thousands of years. This means you can learn about their culture and heritage, especially the indigenous people called Lakota.

You can visit the museum Tatanka to learn the importance bison had for these people or visit Pine Ridge Reservation.

- **I-90 East Region:** The Interstate 90 is 410 miles long. If you drive all those miles, you surely get an idea of the culture and main features of South Dakota!

- **Northern High Plains Region:** Catch a glimpse of the true Old West in the Northern High Plains Region! Visit ranch communities and discover more about the cowboy heritage.

To learn more about each city and region, you can look for information on the official Black Hills and Badlands website www.blackhillsbadlands. com.

Our first journey has come to an end. In the first chapter, we discovered everything we needed about Badlands National Park and some of the surrounding treasures. We looked at basic information about entrance passes and operating hours, and discovered there's no perfect time to visit the park—just the season we enjoy the most. Winter might be the least appropriate time to visit the park due to potential road and accommodation closings so please research closely if this is the season you want to visit in. However, we highly recommend you don't go during summer because of the crowds and high temperatures. We also learned how to get to the park and rent a car, where to sleep, and where to eat. We discovered some interesting breweries and wineries that might come in handy after a picturesque hike. Then, we learned about all the things we can do in the park, like driving through Badlands Loop Road and trying one of the suggested trails. Finally, we looked at surrounding parks, attractions, and cities you might want to visit during your stay. Now, let's keep traveling—Shenandoah National Park is waiting for us!

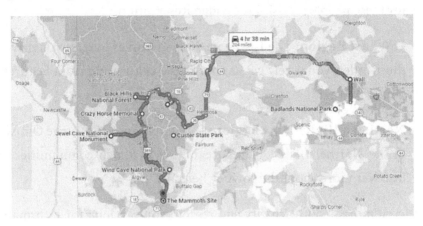

CHAPTER TWO:
SHENANDOAH NATIONAL PARK &
SURROUNDING TREASURES, VIRGINIA

The forest is a quiet place and nature is beautiful. I don't want to sit and rock. I
want to do something." - Emma "Grandma" Gatewood

Have you ever heard of Emma Gatewood? She is considered the
Appalachian Trail's first celebrity because she was the first woman to hike
the whole trail alone (*Emma Gatewood*, n.d.). She was born in 1887 in Ohio
and had 11 children and an abusive husband. When she was 67, she told

her family she would go for a walk, without clarifying that her walk would have started in Maine and ended in Georgia and would have been hundreds of miles long. After a few days on the Appalachian Trail, she realized she was lost. When searchers finally found her, they struggled to convince her to go back home. But that was not the end, as Emma Gatewood decided to go back to the Appalachian Trail after one year and another two times in 1957 and 1964. Now, she's considered a legend for all hikers who want to walk the whole Appalachian Trail (*Emma Gatewood,* n.d.). If you're interested in knowing more about Emma Gatewood, you can also read the book entitled *Grandma Gatewood's Walk: The Inspiring Story of the Woman Who Saved the Appalachian Trail,* written by Ben Montgomery.

Part of the Appalachian Trail crosses Shenandoah National Park, which is situated in the Blue Ridge Mountains of Virginia and is known for its stunning views of the mountains that surround the area and its copious hiking trails. The spectacular Appalachian Trail is one of the park's most famous hikes. The park comprises a bit less than 2,000 acres, in which you can find wildlife such as black bears and bobcats as well as many historical and cultural sites (Pattiz, 2023e). Established in 1926, Shenandoah is the first national park entirely formed through buying lands from private owners. Over the decades, businessmen who lived and ran businesses there did their best to preserve the area and transform it into a national park. It's thanks to those amazing people that we can now admire such beauty.

But Shenandoah National Park occupies a special place in our hearts, too. Beatrix had the pleasure of living just a short distance from this park, in Staunton, for six years. While living there, she hiked the famous trails almost every weekend. This park boasts a landscape that is luscious, romantic, and full of winding paths with waterfalls, rivers, creeks, valleys, wildlife, and mountain views. You could spend months here and not run out of things to explore. Zia visited the park several times, her children in tow, from New York City. Each time they took to the trails, Zia's kids especially enjoyed romping through the creeks and searching for and identifying the wildlife that is always plentiful in the park. Some of our best family memories were made here.

One of the most fascinating aspects of Shenandoah is how the landscape changes over the different seasons. In spring and summer, the area is covered in vibrant shades of green, while in fall it boasts a wide array of autumnal awesomeness—gold, rust, pink, and red, and in winter it is stark and beautifully gloomy. Never a bad time to visit!

Basic Information

Location

Shenandoah National Park has four entrance stations. You will find a variety of places to dine, shop and lodge within minutes of each of these entrance stations. Check out each town's tourism website, provided in this chapter, for more detailed information.

- **Front Royal:** It's the north entrance and is situated near Front Royal, off Route 340, also known as Stonewall Jackson Highway. The address is 21073 Skyline Drive, Front Royal.

- **Rockfish Gap:** It's the south entrance and is situated a few miles east of Waynesboro off of Highway 250. The address is 282 Skyline Drive,

Waynesboro.

- **Swift Run Gap:** It's situated east of Elkton off of US 33. The address is 22591 Spotswood Trail, Elkton.

- **Thornton Gap:** It's situated east of Luray and west of Sperryville off Highway 211, also called Lee Highway. The address is 31339 Skyline Drive, Luray.

Entrance Passes

To visit this special park, you must pay a fee. If you decide to buy one of the interagency passes discussed at the beginning of Chapter 1, you can use them to also see this area because they're valid for all the national parks of the USA. Alternatively, you can buy a pass to visit just Shenandoah. The Standard Entrance Pass costs between $15.00 and $30.00 depending on whether you have a vehicle or not, and which type. Alternatively, you can pay $55.00 to get the Annual Entrance Pass, which allows you to visit the park whenever you want within one year from the moment you buy the pass (*Fees & Passes - Shenandoah National Park*, 2023).

Operating Hours and Seasons

Shenandoah National Park is always open, although you might find Skyline Drive closed in case of severe weather. The Skyline Drive is the only public road that crosses the park, but you can still access the area on foot (*Operating Dates & Hours - Shenandoah National Park*, 2023).
The park has two visitor centers: Dickey Ridge and Byrd. Dickey Ridge is located in the northern area of the park and is easy to access from Front Royal. However, we suggest you visit the official website of the National Park Service before going because the visitor centers aren't always open.

In spring and fall, Dickey Ridge might be closed during certain weekdays, and is always closed during winter. Summer is the only season when they're open every day. Byrd is at the center of the national park. It's always closed in spring and only open during certain weekdays in winter. In both visitor centers, you'll find restrooms, rangers available to answer your questions, an information desk, maps, and bookstores. For more information, you can call (540) 999-3500.

Best Times to Visit

The best times to visit the park are fall and spring. Between September and November, temperatures range between 60-50 °F and 40-30 °F, and an array of red, gold, and orange colors the park (*Best Times to Visit Shenandoah National Park*, n.d.). However, this is also one of the busiest periods in the park, so you might prefer going between March and May. You can still find crowds, but it's less likely because of the changing temperatures. In fact, they can range from 40 °F to 60 °F, with some days at 70 °F. If you want to go during spring, make sure you bring different types of clothes with you—including a raincoat, as showers of rain might occur! A bit of extra preparation is worth it because spring is the most charming season in the park: Wildflowers blossom all around and migrating birds and other animals cross the area on their way north (*Best Times to Visit Shenandoah National Park*, n.d.).

As you might guess, the period between June and August is the most chaotic of the year. Plenty of tourists come to visit the park and the average high temperatures are in the mid-70s °F, although they can get as high as 90° F. Summer in Virginia is also particularly humid, so bring a lot of water and sunscreen with you. In general, we suggest you always check the weather before packing for your trip. Conversely, the months between December and February are less crowded due to the low temperatures, which can fall as low as 30 °F. In addition, winter in the park is characterized by storms that make trails strenuous to hike. For this reason, we suggest you visit the park in winter only if you're an expert hiker and know how to properly protect yourself from extreme cold (*Best Times to Visit Shenandoah National Park*, n.d.).

How to Get There

You can arrive at Shenandoah National Park by car or plane.

Car

Depending on the state from which you leave and the entrance you want to arrive at, you can choose one of the following routes (*Directions - Shenandoah National Park*, 2022).

- **Driving From Richmond, Virginia:** To reach Rockfish Gap Entrance, travel west on I-64 to exit 99, and follow signs for the park. To Swift Run Gap Entrance Station, travel west on I-64 to Charlottesville, take exit to US-29 North, and go left onto US-33 West for 14 miles.

- **Driving From Washington, D.C. Metro Area:** To Front Royal Entrance Station, travel west on I-66, exit to Route 340 South, and follow signs for the park. To Thornton Gap Entrance Station, travel west on I-66 to exit 43A. Take US-29 South to Warrenton and then US-211 West.

- **Driving From Pittsburgh, Pennsylvania:** To reach Front Royal

Entrance Station, travel east on I-76 to exit 161. Take I-70 East to US-522 South, follow VA-37 South to I-81 South, then I-81 South to I-66 East, and take the latter route to get to the park.

Plane

You can reach the park from four different airports, which are all pretty close.

- **Washington Dulles International:** It's less than 60 miles away from Front Royal Entrance Station.

- **Reagan National:** It's 70 miles east of Front Royal Entrance Station.

- **Shenandoah Valley Regional:** It's less than 30 miles west of Swift Run Gap Entrance Station.

- **Charlottesville-Albemarle:** It's 31 miles away from Rockfish Gap Entrance Station.

All the above airports can get you to Shenandoah National Park and offer you the opportunity to rent a car or RV. If you want an alternative way to get a vehicle to visit the park, you can also use the Turo app, which we discussed in Chapter 1. The app gives you the chance to rent a car from locals, which is an affordable and sustainable solution!

Accommodations

At Shenandoah National Park, you can choose from a vast array of hotels and other accommodations. As mentioned previously, you can always check out each town's tourism website for additional lodging options; like hotels and Bed & Breakfasts, for example!

Best Places to Stay Inside the Park

- **Big Meadows Lodge:** It's at mile 51 of Skyline Drive and inside the heart of the park. In fact, it can be crammed. The main lodge building dates back to 1939 and has all amenities, including a gift shop and a restaurant. This place also has detached cabins, suites, and traditional rooms. Some rooms are also pet-friendly. You can find a campground close to the main lodge. For more information or to book a stay call (855) 584-5292.

- **Skyland Lodge:** It's at mile 41.7 of the Skyline Drive and a breathtaking treasure in the park. This lodge is so old that it was created before the establishment of the Shenandoah National Park, at the end of the 1890s (Bram, 2022)! Here, you can be amazed at the stunning views over the park and enjoy a variety of accommodation options. For more information or to book a stay call (877) 847-1919.

- **Lewis Mountain Cabins:** You can find them at mile 57.5 of the Skyline Drive. These cabins are rustic and quaint, with no internet or phone. However, they offer some basic comforts, like a sheltered picnic table and private bathroom. If you want to try an authentic off-the-grid experience into the wild, then these cabins are for you! Alternatively, you can stay in the campground close to the cabins. For more information or to book a stay call (855) 584-5292.

Best Places to Stay Near the Park

- **Luray Lodging:** Luray is a small city 15 miles away from the park, so it's your best option if you want to be as close to it as you can. Among the many lodging options, you can find in Luray, we recommend two. Hotel Laurance is just a 16-minute drive from the park and one of the most beautiful hotels in the city. If you prefer a more affordable option, you can try Hawksbill House, which is still very close to the park entrance.

- **Front Royal Lodging:** Front Royal is a city situated at the beginning of Skyline Drive, so it's a perfect place to find accommodations close to the park. In this city, you can sleep at Super 8 or Baymont. Super 8 is the perfect location to be close to the park and enjoy the spectacular views of the area. In fact, it's just a 3-minute drive away from the Front Royal Entrance. It also has a room for every budget. Baymont also has many room options and some advantages: Your stay includes free breakfast, Wi-Fi, and parking.

- **Harrisonburg Lodging:** Harrisonburg is a 35-minute drive from the Swift Run Gap Entrance and offers a wide variety of lodging options. Cave Hill Farm Bed & Breakfast is a historic manor that was built in the 1930s and has five guest rooms available. Alternatively, Hyatt Place Harrisonburg provides luxury facilities for a fairly reasonable price. Here, you have everything you need and more, from a swimming pool to a fitness center. (White Oak Lavender Farm is a must visit activity if in this area, btw! A personal favorite.)

- **Waynesboro North 340 Campground:** It's only 38 minutes away from the Rockfish Gap Entrance Station and provides an RV park. For more information, you can call (540) 943-9573. You can also access a full list of additional lodging options in and around the town of Waynesboro at: www.visitwaynesboro.com under "lodging".

- **Spacious Skies Shenandoah Views:** A campground located in Luray and is a very peaceful and quiet rural area. For more information, you can call (540) 743-7222.

Look at the website or contact the above places to find out which one best satisfies your needs and desires. Also, keep in mind you can always find a comfortable place with Airbnb or Vrbo near each service station, which we already mentioned in the previous chapter. Just scroll their website or download their app to choose the perfect spot for you.

Restaurants

Inside the park, you can find a place to stop and grab something to eat every 25 miles, so you won't struggle to find satisfying meals (*Dining - Shenandoah National Park*, 2021).

- **Skyland:** At mile 41.7 and 42.5, you can find three options to satisfy your appetite. *Pollock Dining Room* is a complete restaurant that provides breakfast, lunch, and dinner. If you are looking for something faster or snacks, you can go to *Grab 'n Go. Mountain Taproom* is perfect for nightly family-friendly entertainment and to grab a beer or a glass of wine.

- **Loft Mountain Wayside:** At mile 79.5 there's *Loft Mountain Wayside*, which provides breakfast, grilled food, and sandwiches.

- **Big Meadows Wayside:** At mile 51.2 you can sit down to eat your meal or grab something to eat during your visit inside the park.

- **Big Meadows Lodge:** Also at mile 51.2, you can find the *New Market Taproom* and *Spottswood Dining Room*. The first one offers you the opportunity to quickly grab lunch on the go, sit outside with your fur friend, and taste specialty drinks. *Spottswood Dining Room* is more rustic.

- **Elkwallow Wayside:** It's at mile 24.1 and provides breakfast, sandwiches, and grilled meals.

Goods and Services

You will probably need to fill the tank, park your vehicle, find a spot with internet connection from time to time, or buy a souvenir for a friend or relative. Here you find a complete list of goods and services close to the park (*Goods & Services - Shenandoah National Park*, 2023).

- **Gasoline:** Make sure to plan your trip carefully, as there's only one gas station inside the park and it's not 100% reliable due to frequent power outages. It's at mile 51, Big Meadows Wayside.

- **Electric Vehicle Charging Station:** Plug-in hybrids and electric vehicles can be freely charged at Byrd Visitor Center at mile 51 and Skyland at mile 41.7 and 42.5.

- **Bike Repair Station:** If you want to visit the park by bike and need to repair it, you can go to Skyland at miles 41.7 and 42.5, Elkwallow Wayside at mile 24, and Loft Mountain at mile 79.5.

- **Park Stores:** Park stores sell books, souvenirs, maps, clothing, and much more. You can find them at both visitor centers of the park (Dickey Ridge and Byrd).

- **Camp stores:** You can buy groceries and camping supplies at all of the four camp stores inside the park. You can find them at Loft Mountain Camp store (mile 79.5), Elkwallow Wayside (mile 24),

Lewis Mountain Camp store (mile 57.6), and Big Meadows Wayside (mile 51).

- **Internet & Cellular Access:** Cell coverage is absent in most areas of the park except for the Dickey Ridge visitor center and some overlooks on the west side of the area. You'll also find free Wi-Fi at Byrd visitor center, Skyland Dining Room, and Big Meadows Lodge.

- **Gift Shop:** Do you want to buy some souvenirs or gifts for your loved ones who couldn't come on this amazing journey with you? You can go to Elkwallow Wayside (mile 24), Loft Mountain Wayside (mile 79.5), Skyland (miles 41.7 and 42.5), and Big Meadows Lodge and Wayside (both at mile 51).

Shops, Groceries, or Markets Nearby

Do you need to stock up on groceries and other necessities? Here are some options near Shenandoah National Park below.

- **Shenandoah IGA:** Finding a grocery store near Skyline Drive isn't easy, but you can go to *Shenandoah IGA*, which is a little more than 10 miles away. There, you'll find all the basics you might need at a reasonable price. The store is at 607 S 3rd St Shenandoah, 22849. For more information, you can call (540) 652-8261.

- **Food Lion:** The *Food Lion* is pretty well-stocked and reliable grocery store. You can find all sorts of food items and travel necessities here. Located at 14811 Spotswood Trl Elkton, 22827 or you can call (540) 298-9455 for more information.

- **Dollar General:** This store provides all sorts of items at very low prices. In addition to common food and snacks, you can find health and beauty aids, seasonal items, cleaning supplies, and family apparel. The store is at 727 4TH ST Shenandoah, 22849. You can call (540) 918-0212.

- **The Valley Pantry & Deli:** There, you can find high-quality and delicious food that will blow your mind! The store is at 15451 Old Spotswood Trl Elkton, 22827. For more information, you can call (540) 298-1057.

- **The Market at Massanutten Station:** If you stay at the Massanutten resort and don't want to go to the *Food Lion*, which is the closest store, you can still go to the *Market*. There, you'll find everything you need at a reasonable price. The store is at 1850 Meadow Vista Ln Massanutten, 22840. For more information, you can call (540) 289-4098.

- **Kite Store:** The store provides delicious sandwiches, beers, and other supplies. Located at 4258 US Highway 340 Shenandoah, 22849. For more information, you can call (540) 652-8174.

- **Ciro's Italian Eatery:** If you long for Italian food, you should absolutely go to *Ciro's*! The food and service are excellent—you won't be disappointed. Located at 101 Downey Knoll Elkton, 22827. For more information, you can call (540) 298-1205.

Breweries and Wineries

After a long but exciting day of hiking and sightseeing, you might need to refresh, relax, and recharge your batteries with a good craft beer or bottle of wine. Shenandoah National Park doesn't fall short when it comes to excellent breweries and wineries!

- **Skyline Brewing:** Located at 72 Christmas Tree Ln, Washington.

- **Vibrissa Beer:** Located at 122 E. Main St, Front Royal.

- **Cave Hills Farm Brewing:** Located at 1001 Jacob Burner Dr, McGaheysville.

- **Elkton Brewing:** Located at 100 N. 5th Street, Elkton.

- **Seven Arrows Brewing:** Located at 2508 Jefferson Hwy #1, Waynesboro.

- **Basic City Beer Co.:** Located just minutes from the Rockfish Gap entrance at 1010 E. Main St., Waynesboro.

- **Queen City Brewing:** Located at 834 Spring Hill Rd, Staunton.

- **Red Beard Brewing:** Located at 120 S Lewis St, Staunton.

- **Chester Gap Cellars:** Located at 4615 Remount Rd, Front Royal.

- **Little Washington Winery:** Located at 65 Clark Ln, Washington.

- **Wisteria Farm and Vineyard:** Located at 1126 Marksville Rd, Stanley.

- **Muse Vineyards:** Located at 16 Serendipity Ln, Woodstock.

This is by no means an exhaustive list. Check out the tourism websites for the cities and towns you are closest to for an even greater selection of destinations. They are all quite good! You will definitely be pleased.

Rules and Regulations

If you plan to visit a national park with your pet, Shenandoah is the one you should choose, as it's one of the few national parks that allows you to bring your pet with you on the trails. Remember, you're responsible for your own pet, so you must bring enough water for them, feed them, and bag their waste. You can bring your fur friend everywhere except on Ranger Programs and you must always keep it on a leash less than six feet long. Be advised however that pets are not allowed on specific trails (*Pets - Shenandoah National Park*, 2022).

For a full list of any park rules and regulations concerning pets and the trails where they're allowed, visit www.nps.gov.

History and Trivia

As you already learned in the introduction, Shenandoah National Park is the first national park that was completely formed by lands bought from private owners. However, the park hides some more interesting facts. Close to the park, remains of prehistoric creatures have been found (Pattiz, 2023e). In particular, around 200 mastodon bones were excavated less than 3 hours away from the park. Remains of mammoths have also been found. Interestingly, President Thomas Jefferson collected some of the bones he found in the area and tried to figure out where they came from.

As with Badlands National Park, Shenandoah has also been the Native Americans' home for millennia (Pattiz, 2023e). People have been living there for more than 9,000 years, especially Woodland tribes.

Scenic Drives and Overlooks

Scenic views are literally everywhere inside the park, so you won't struggle to find an amazing spot to enjoy the panorama. From Skyline Drive, you can reach breathtaking viewpoints, which we'll look at below.

- **Tunnel Parking Overlook:** South of Thornton Gap Entrance, you can find three overlooks which are just half a mile away from each other. The first one is Tunnel Parking, which is named after the tunnel that lies next to it.

- **Buck Hollow Overlook:** This is the second overlook and is a bit more special than the other two because of its stunning views over the park during sunrise. It also provides a wider and more open glimpse at the area.

- **Hazel Mountain Overlook:** This is the third overlook and it derives its name from Hazel Mountain, which can be easily spotted from there.

- **Ivy Creek Overlook:** Be amazed by the picturesque ridges of the park that you'll be able to see from this viewpoint!

- **Hazeltop Ridge Overlook:** This is a classic view that allows you to look at the area from the southwest to the northwest.

- **Sawmill Run Overlook:** The vista is awesome especially from spring to fall!

- **The Oaks Overlook:** It offers you a glimpse at the valley below the park—an alternative view over the area.

- **Spitler Knoll Overlook:** It's one of the longest views and provides one of the widest panoramic perspectives on the park.

- **The Point Overlook:** We absolutely recommend you see this one! You can stay in the parking area or walk for just a few minutes to enjoy the breathtaking scenery.

- **Rockytop Overlook:** From here you'll see both the typical ridges and mountains of the park and the valley beyond them.

But that's not all! Inside the park, you'll find 10 additional overlooks. For more information, don't hesitate to look at www.nps.gov or go to a visitor center once you're there.

Things to Do in the Park

Enjoy the magic and splendor of Shenandoah National Park by doing a few of the things listed below

- **Blue Ridge Mountain Views:** No matter where you are in Shenandoah, you'll always have the chance to gaze at the spectacular Blue Ridge Mountains. The scenery is especially magical during fall.

- **Sunrises and sunsets:** Watching the sun rise or dip behind the Blue Ridge Mountains is just beyond words.

- **Waterfalls:** There are 10 amazing waterfalls, although most of them are on moderate or even strenuous trails.

- **Miles and miles of hiking trails:** If you're an expert hiker or love walking surrounded by nature, this park is perfect for you. There, you'll find more than 500 miles of hiking trails.

- **Wildlife watching:** The total number of animal species is still unknown, but there are surely a lot (Bram, 2020). You may find more than 30 species of fish, 50 different types of mammals, and 50 species of reptiles and amphibians. Among the mammals, you may spot the famous black bears, coyotes and bobcats, and white-tailed deer.

- **Scenic Skyline Drive:** As you discovered in the previous section, Skyline Drive is full of breathtaking overlooks. Just drive and enjoy the jaw dropping views.

- **Big Meadows:** From the Byrd visitor center, you can easily reach Big Meadows, which is a huge grassland at the center of the park. It was previously a farmland, and now it's full of wildflowers and animals attracted by them, like the black bear.

- **Mountain mist:** The Blue Ridge Mountains are filled with mystery and ancient wisdom that can be physically perceived after a rainstorm or during a cold spring morning when the mist rises from the ground.

Hiking Trails

Having more than 500 miles at your disposal means choosing the right hiking trail is not that simple. You will find some of the most beautiful hikes below, from the easiest to the most difficult.

- **Blackrock Summit via Trayfoot Mountain and Appalachian Trail:** It's an easy loop of a bit more than one mile. It's flat and gives you the chance to look at stunning views over the park.

- **Blackrock and Appalachian Trail Loop at Big Meadows:** It's an easy loop of less than one mile that takes more or less 25 minutes to complete.

- **Rose River Trail:** It's a 3.8-mile loop trail that is moderately difficult. You'll have to walk for two hours but you'll have the chance to glimpse some amazing waterfalls.

- **Stony Man via Appalachian Trail:** It's a 1.5-mile loop trail that is considered moderate. Although it takes less than an hour to complete it, it's characterized by ascents.

- **Hawksbill Loop Trail:** It's a loop of 2.6 miles that is considered a moderate hike. The terrain is steep and rocky and it takes more or less one hour and a half to complete the trail. When you reach the highest point of the hike, you'll see the park from above—absolutely worth the effort!

Surrounding Treasures

To take a break from the wild and discover hidden treasures around the park, we absolutely recommend you visit some of the places below.

- **Barren Ridge Vineyards:** It's a winery that has been managed by the same family for generations. It provides a lot of fun activities to do and wines to taste! It's also one of our favorites. The best wine there is Red Barren: A luscious red served both chilled and at room temp. The address is 984 Barren Ridge Rd Fishersville, 22939. To ask for more information and book a tasting, you can call (540) 248-3300.

- **New River Gorge National Park:** If you want to visit the three main areas of New River Gorge National Park (Canyon Rim, Grand View, and Sandstone) and have enough time to go white water rafting, you will likely need a minimum of three days. On the website www.earthtrekker.com, you can find options for one to three-day itineraries. New River Gorge National Park is just a three-hour drive from Shenandoah but so worth it. This area is one of our favorite places to cycle, tube, and kayak in the summer. So thrilled it has recently been made a national park! Among the main attractions, there's the renowned suspension bridge, which is one of America's highest (*Welcome to the Royal Gorge Bridge & Park*, n.d.). For more information, you can visit the website www.royalgorgebridge.com.

- **Front Royal:** It's the northern gateway to the park and a little town that provides a lot of outdoor fun, like rafting, kayaking, golfing, and horseback riding. The town is also full of restaurants, boutiques, and museums that tell the story of the Civil War. For more information, you can visit www.discoverfrontroyal.com.

- **Luray:** The main reason you should visit Luray is its famous caverns, which are the largest in the whole of the USA. (Kennedy, 2021). In addition, the town is characterized by 19th-century buildings and one-of-a-kind shops. For more information, you can visit www. townofluray.com.

- **Waynesboro:** This special little valley town is the spot where the Appalachian Trail, Shenandoah National Park, and the Blue Ridge

Mountains intersect. There, you can fly fish in the South River 365 days a year, walk or cycle the 2-mile South River Greenway Trail, picnic in Constitution Park, and taste craft beers and delicious wines in unique settings, just to name a few things. For more information, you can visit www.visitwaynesboro.com.

- **Staunton:** Last but not least, Staunton is the oldest town west of the Blue Ridge Mountains and was virtually untouched during the Civil War due to its high number of entertainment venues, bars, and brothels at the time. An incredibly historic town in the heart of the Shenandoah Valley, with the most charming downtown you will ever see. The perfect place to spend a few days shopping for local treasures, hitting a ghost tour or a museum or two, catching a show at the Shakespeare Theater, eating farm-to-table meals, or visiting a few breweries! Staunton is incredibly beautiful and regularly listed as one of the most charming towns in the USA. There is much to do! Beatrix lived here for six years and it was hands down the best place she ever lived. Among the activities to do in town, you can try the glass blowing studio, the Frontier Culture Museum, theaters, shops, restaurants, wine tasting, and in-town breweries. For more information, you can visit www.visitstaunton.com.

In this chapter, we have gathered all the information you need to enjoy your time at Shenandoah National Park and discover some of the surrounding treasures. You have basic information about the four entrances, the two visitor centers, and contact information to learn more about the park. The best times to visit the park are spring and fall, and you can get there by car or plane. Then, you can sleep inside the park or choose from a variety of lodging options in one of the nearby cities. We also discussed useful information about where to eat, buy groceries, fill the tank, access the internet, and much more. Next, we looked at 10 of the 20 most scenic overlooks inside the park which cross Skyline Drive, the main road of the park. We also discussed exciting things you can do and some of the easiest and moderate trails you shouldn't miss. Finally, we mentioned some hidden gems you can find close to the park. Now, it's time to leave Shenandoah and head to Capitol Reef!

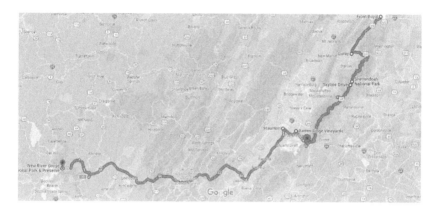

CHAPTER THREE:
CAPITOL REEF NATIONAL PARK &
SURROUNDING TREASURES, UTAH

Always be on the lookout for the presence of wonder. -E.B. White

Established in 1971, Capitol Reef National Park is located in the State of Utah and covers an area of more than 200,000 acres (Pattiz, 2023g). Its main attraction is the stunning scenery made up of deep canyons, red rock cliffs, and geological features. The park is also famous for its culturally and historically relevant sites. The park has been the home of different communities for thousands of years (Pattiz, 2023g).

Why would you want to visit Capitol Reef? Just driving through this scenic park makes your heart swell with joy! We recall stopping to take many, many photos (some featured in this chapter) on our drive through this nothing-short-of-stunning landscape. Have your cameras or phones ready folks! Zia and Beatrix both agree that their roadside picnic lunch here was a clear favorite when compared to all of their past scenic picnics and that is saying something. There is a small museum in this park and it is next to a horse pasture with an incredible view. We had a blast feeding one of the horses apples and carrots. Life is full of simple pleasures and moments to be grateful for and that was definitively one of them.

Basic Information

Location

52 West Headquarters Drive, Torrey, UT 84775.

Entrance Passes

The entrance fee varies from $10.00 to $20.00 depending on whether you just need a ticket to visit the park on foot or you are entering with a private vehicle (*Basic Information - Capitol Reef National Park*, 2022). Alternatively, you can get the annual entrance pass at $35.00. This way, you can visit the park whenever you want within a year from the moment you buy the pass. As always, the interagency passes discussed in Chapter 1 are also valid for this park.

Alternatively, you can also buy a digital pass before arriving in the park. You just have to visit www.recreation.gov and get yours (*Fees & Passes - Capitol Reef National Park*, 2023)! Capitol Reef National Park also requires a free permit to backpack and practice canyoneering, rock climbing, and bouldering. For more information, you can look at the National Park Service website www.nps.gov.

Operating Hours and Contact Information

The park is open all year and you'll find only one visitor center which is open every day except for some major holidays (*Operating Hours & Seasons - Capitol Reef National Park*, 2023). The visitor center provides everything visitors need to get more information about the park, exhibits, and a museum that gives many insights into the history, geology, and archaeology of the area. For more information on operating hours, you can call (435) 425-3791.

Campgrounds are open all year but they're first come, first served, from November to February and must be reserved from March to October. For more information and to make a reservation, you can visit www. recreation.gov (*Permits & Reservations - Capitol Reef National Park*, 2023).

Best Times to Visit

The best times to visit Capitol Reef are spring and fall, which are also the busiest seasons because the weather is perfect for hiking and backpacking. There's more chance of snow and dangerously heavy rains during winter, so it's not an ideal time to visit the park. In general, it's always better to check weather and road conditions in advance. The most crowded but also amazing months in which you should visit the park are September and October, and from March to June (*Visiting During the Busy Season - Capitol Reef National Park*, 2022).

You might wonder how you can enjoy your visit amidst chaos and traffic. Well, you can follow some easy tips. First, visiting the park during the week is better because crowds tend to pile up on the weekend. Second, you must be flexible about the trails you want to try and when you want to visit the park. If a hike is full of people, you can choose another one. In addition, people amass during the day while you can find some quiet early in the morning or late in the evening. Take advantage of those moments to enjoy a breathtaking sunrise or sunset inside the park. Finally, you can choose less visited areas, like the South and North districts, which are still worth it!

How to Get There

Car

- **Interstate 70:** If you travel westbound, follow I-70 to exit 149, then take Utah State Route 24 toward Hanksville and continue for 43.8 miles. Then, turn right and continue for 37.3 miles when you'll reach the Capitol Reef Visitor Center. If you travel eastbound, follow I-70 to exit 40, then turn right onto Utah State Route 120 and continue for 1.2 miles. Turn left onto Utah State Route 118 north/ E 300 N and continue for 0.8 miles until you reach Utah State Route 119 east and continue for 8.8 miles. Turn right onto Utah State Route 24 and continue for 63.4 miles when you'll reach the visitor center of the park.

- **Interstate 15:** If you travel northbound, follow I-15 north to exit 95 then take Utah State Route 20 and continue for 20.4 miles. Turn left onto US-89 north, turn right onto Utah State Route 62, turn left onto Utah State Route 62, then turn right onto Utah State Route 24 east and continue until you see the Capitol Reef Visitor Center. If you travel southbound, follow I-15 south to exit 188, take US-50 east and turn left onto Utah State Route 50. Turn right onto US-50 east/ North State Street, turn right onto Utah State Route 260 south, then turn right onto Utah State Route 24 (SR-24) east and continue for about 74 miles. Then, you'll find the visitor center on your right.

- **Utah State Route 12:** It's convenient if you plan to visit Bryce Canyon and then go on to Capitol Reef. The parks are about three hours apart.

Plane

- **Salt Lake City:** If you want, you can take a flight to Salt Lake City.

From there, you can reach Capitol Reef National Park in four different ways. You can fly to Moab and then drive for less than three hours. You can fly to Cedar City, take a bus to Richfield, and then drive for approximately one hour and 40 minutes. The journey is about six hours in total. Alternatively, you can fly to St. George Regional, take the bus to Richfield, then drive to Capitol Reef. You can also take the bus directly from Salt Lake City to Richfield.

- **St. George Regional:** From St. George Regional Airport you can reach the park by bus and car in about five hours.

- **Provo:** Provo Airport is a bit further away than Salt Lake City and St. George Regional to the national park. You can take the bus from there and reach Capitol Reef in about nine hours.

- **Grand Junction:** From Grand Junction, it also takes nine hours to reach the park. From there, you can take the bus and shuttle to Richfield.

As you might have already noticed, you need a car to reach Capitol Reef. You can rent one at the airport, use the Turo app we already discussed, or rent an RV through www.outdoorsy.com, which is a reliable source. Just visit the website and find the best RV for you.

Accommodations

Capitol Reef National Park offers plenty of accommodations for all tastes! You'll find a list of the most recommended places below.

- **Fruita Campground:** It's the only developed campground in the park. It's open from March to October and only has 71 spaces, so you must make a reservation. To book a spot, you can visit www.

recreation.gov.

- **Cathedral Valley Campground:** It's a primitive campground 36 miles away from the visitor center. It only has six spots and water is not available. It's first come, first served. As it's difficult to reach, you must check road conditions before going.

- **Cedar Mesa Campground:** It's the other primitive campground inside the park and is 23 miles away from Utah State Highway 24. It only has five spots and water isn't available.

- **The Broken Spur Inn:** Just five minutes from the park entrance, this hotel provides a steakhouse, a pool and tub, classical rooms, and the opportunity to spend the night in one of their Conestoga wagons. That's a real Old West experience! For more information and to book a stay, you can call (435) 425-3775.

- **The Rim Rock Inn & Restaurants:** It's located in Torrey and offers an authentic atmosphere with a rustic setting. Accommodations are comfortable and prices are more affordable than in other hotels and glamping areas. For more information and to book a stay, you can call (435) 425-3398.

- **Red Sands Hotel:** It's located in Torrey and provides a variety of suites and rooms. It also has a spa that allows you to relax after a long walk! For more information and to book a stay, you can call (435) 425-3688.

- **The Lodge at Red River Ranch:** It's located on Utah Highway 24, just outside the gate of Capitol Reef. *The Lodge* has an architecture that evokes the Old West and is a luxury hotel. It provides a room where guests can gather and relax, and has guest rooms. The staff of the hotel also raise bison, so you can see them roam and take pictures. For more information and to book a stay, you can call (435) 425-3322.

- **Cougar Ridge Lodge:** It's located in Torrey, a little bit off the beaten path. The place provides the Grand Lodge for families or big groups of people and luxury villas—most of which are pet friendly! For more information and to book a stay, you can call (435) 680-9170.

As always, remember to also check Airbnb and Vrbo to find the perfect accommodation for you.

Restaurants

You can have a tasty meal in the hotels and accommodations listed above. But what if you're looking for something different? Here are some delicious restaurants you can find in the cities close to the park.

- **Sunglow Family Restaurant:** The address is 91 East Main, Bicknell, 84715. This restaurant is open all year and perfect for families. The specialties include Mexican food, steaks, and burgers. For more information, you can call (435) 425-3701.

- **Stan's Burger Shak:** The address is 150 UT-95, Hanksville. It's open all year and provides exquisite home-made food, like onion rings. For more information, you can call (435) 542-3330.

- **Marinia's Country Cafe:** The address is 289 North Main, Loa. It's open all year and provides breakfast all day. It's famous for its homemade food, like pies and soups. For more information, you can call (435) 836-2047.

- **Cliffstone Restaurant:** The address is 2900 W. Highway 24, Teasdale. It's located at the Red River Ranch and open seasonally. For more information and to reserve a table, you can call (435) 425-3322.

- **Austin's Chuckwagon Deli:** The address is 12 West Main, Torrey. It serves homemade food, quality meals, and daily specials. You can eat sandwiches, Mexican food, or wraps. For more information, you can call (435) 425-3290.

- **Broken Spur Steakhouse:** The address is 955 East Highway 24 Torrey. There, you can get a box lunch if you want to eat outside or have a meal inside the restaurant. The menu includes chicken, steak, and vegetarian food. For more information, you can call (435) 425-3775.

- **Pioneer Kitchen:** The address is 2600 East Highway 24, Torrey. It's located inside Capitol Reef Resort and only open for breakfast and dinner. For more information, you can call (435) 425-3323.

- **Rim Rock Restaurant:** The address is 2523 East Highway 24, Torrey. If you want a taste of the Old West, that's the place! You can enjoy your meal while gazing at a 360-degree view of Capitol Reef. For more information, you can call (435) 425-3388.

- **Slacker's Burger Joint:** The address is 65 East Main, Torrey. It's open from March to October and famous for its burgers, that are among the most delicious in all Utah! For more information, you can call (435) 425-3710.

Gas Stations

If you need to fill the tank while traveling through Capitol Reef, here are the best and closest gas stations.

- **Phillips 66 Gas Station:** Located at 675 E Highway 24, Torrey.

- **Sinclair Gas:** Located at 877 Highway 24, Torrey.

- **Taft Travel Plaza #2:** Located at 351 UT-24, Bicknell and it's open 24/7.

- **Hidden Falls Market:** Located at address is 241 North Main St, Loa.

Shops, Groceries, or Markets Nearby

Among the shops and grocery stores you can find close to Capitol Reef, there are certainly many Family Dollar stores and a Walmart. You can find a Family Dollar in Loa (S Main St 75), Salina (S State St 22), Gunnison (S Main St 433), and Panguitch (N Main St 535). You'll find a Walmart at E 1300 S 10, Richfield. Alternatively, you can go to the following stores:

- **Royal's Food Town:** 135 W Main St, Loa and open every day. For more information, you can call (435) 836-2841.

- **Bull Mountain Market:** 30 E 100th N, Hanksville and open every day except Sunday. For more information, you can call (435) 542-3249.

- **Chuck Wagon General:** 12 W Main St, Torrey and open every day. For more information, you can call (435) 425-3288.

Breweries and Wineries

Part of the journey includes relaxing at sunset while drinking a good glass of wine, spirits, or beer while taking in the amazing landscapes of Capitol Reef. You find a few of the best breweries and wineries worth a visit below.

- **Etta Place Cider:** Located at 700 W Main St, Torrey.

- **Silver Reef Brewery & Distillery:** Located at 4391 Enterprise Drive, St. George.

- **Water Canyon Winery:** Located at 1050 Field Ave, Hildale.

- **New World Distillery:** Located at 4795 2600 N, Eden.

Rules and Regulations

Capitol Reef National Park has some specific rules and regulations you must follow. You can sleep at night in your vehicle or camp only in the allowed campgrounds, which are Fruita, Cathedral Valley, and Cedar Mesa. You can't use drones inside the park, leave scratches or drawings on the rocks, use firearms, or hunt wild animals. In addition, you need a permit to backpack overnight and for some activities, like canyoneering, rock climbing, and bouldering. You also need permits and reservations for large groups, weddings, guided tours, and commercial filming. For more information, you can visit the website www.nps.gov (*Regulations - Capitol Reef National Park*, 2023).

What about our fur friends? You can bring your pet with you, but it must always be on a six-feet leash and is not allowed in many areas inside the park, including hiking trails, public buildings, and campgrounds. For more information, you can visit www.nps.gov (*Pets - Capitol Reef National Park*, 2022).

History and Trivia

Let's look at some of the most fascinating historical facts linked with Capitol Reef, starting a millennia ago.

In the introduction to this chapter, we already mentioned people lived there for thousands of years. The first known people to call Capitol Reef home were the Fremont people, who lived there around year 700 (*Capitol Reef History*, n.d.). We also know for sure that between 1600 and 1800 the Paiute tribes lived in Capitol Reef, until early pioneers pressured them to leave.

Once settlers started to arrive, they called the area Wayne County and organized the Wayne Wonderland Club to protect and preserve the environment. Years later, settlers considered the opportunity to establish a national park and thought to call it "Wayne Wonderland State Park." But not all of them agreed, as some believed Capitol Reef was a much better name (Pattiz, 2023g).

So, where does the name "Capitol Reef" come from? Capitol Reef is the name that early pioneers gave to the white domes of Navajo sandstone, which resemble the dome of the Capitol building in Washington, DC (Pattiz, 2023g). They thought Capitol Reef represented the unusual geography of the area, so they thought it was the perfect name.

Scenic Drives and Overlooks

Now, you might wonder where you should stop to enjoy the views and get the best out of your trip to Capitol Reef. You'll find a list of the most scenic overlooks below.

- **Burr Trail Loop/Burr Point Trail:** This place is accessible by vehicle, although you might struggle with an RV. Head south from Hanksville, turn left at mile marker 15.5, and go to Burr Point Road. Then, follow signs east 11 miles until you reach a place with many spots to park your vehicle. There, you'll enjoy the view of the Dirty Devil River Canyon, which is 1,400 feet deep. The sight is certainly

70

worth the effort!

- **Cathedral Valley:** It's a 5.8-mile loop that starts at River Ford and ends at Caineville. Along the road, you'll see stark desert vistas, monoliths, and panoramic views.

- **Fishlake Scenic Byway:** If you're passionate about fishing or just want to see some wildlife, you must try this route. Take Utah SR 24 20 miles north of Loa, then follow the signs to the Fishing Recreation Area. To fish, you can stop at Johnson Reservoir or Fish Lake. Along the way, you might spot elk, moose, and mountain lions.

- **Aquarius Plateau:** It's a 46-mile road from Bicknell to Escalante or 58-mile route from Bicknell to Boulder. Aquarius Plateau is a surprising breathtaking adventure you must try!

- **The North Slope Road:** It takes you up Boulder Mountain where you'll enjoy scenic views of the surrounding countryside and will probably spot some wild animals, like marmots or mule deer.

- **Scenic Highway 12:** Just follow Highway 12 and admire the area. You can use it to go from Capitol Reef to Bryce Canyon and vice versa.

- **Hogan Pass Overlook:** It's absolutely a must as it is more than 9,000 feet above the sea level and allows you to look out over Cathedral Valley. You can literally see hundreds of miles away, so make sure to bring binoculars with you.

Things to Do in the Park

In addition to visiting the area by car and enjoying various overlooks, you can do many other things inside the park.

- **Horseback riding:** Horses are allowed in all areas except a few designated ones.

- **Wildlife viewing:** Inside the park, you may glimpse many animals you won't find elsewhere, such as ringtails, antelope squirrels, and yellow-bellied marmots.

- **Rock climbing:** The local rocks are mainly sandstone which can be flaky. If you want to go rock climbing or bouldering, remember to check the climbing zones first.

- **Ranger programs:** Rangers offer a variety of programs and organize all sorts of events throughout the year, like watching the stars at night or learning about the geologic history of the area. All those programs are perfect for kids – big and small!

- **Waterpocket district:** If you're looking for a real adventure, you must go to the Waterpocket district. It's rugged and remote, and open all year. Just make sure to check weather conditions before going.

- **Fruita:** It's the heart of Capitol Reef National Park and offers the opportunity to learn more about the geologic and human history of the area, and enjoy amazing landscapes.

For specific information about the above activities, you can visit www. nps.gov.

Hiking Trails

Among all the things you can do, there's obviously hiking! You find a list with the most popular and spectacular trails below.

- **Goosenecks:** It's a 0.1-mile easy trail that provides breathtaking views over the canyons.

- **Sunset Point:** It's a 0.4-mile easy hike that is perfect for enjoying the sunset and taking wonderful pictures of Capitol Reef.

- **Capitol Gorge:** It's a one-mile easy hike that allows you to look at deep canyons and historic inscriptions.

- **Cohab Canyon:** It's a 1.7 moderate trail that provides amazing views of Fruita and stunning overlooks over the park and hidden canyons.

- **Hickman Bridge:** It's a 0.9-mile moderate hike that leads you to an impressive 133-foot natural bridge. Incredible!

- **Navajo Nobs:** It's a 4.7-mile strenuous trail that provides 360-degree mountaintop panoramas.

Suggested Itineraries

What if you only have a limited amount of time to visit Capitol Reef? You can choose a different itinerary depending on how long you plan to stay.

One or Two Hours

- Stop at the visitor center and watch the park movie *Watermark*, also available online.

- Take a short hike, such as Hickman Bridge.

- Tour the Scenic Drive (approximately 90 minutes round trip).

- Visit the petroglyph panel, historic schoolhouse, or the Gifford House Store and Museum to enjoy fresh-baked pie when in season!

- Pick some delicious fruit when in season.

- Join a ranger for a program.

One Day

- Take a longer hike, such as Cohab Canyon or Chimney Rock.

- Join a ranger-guided walk, talk, evening program or astronomy program.

- Become a Junior Ranger. Booklets are available at the visitor center.

- Tour the North District/Cathedral Valley (often HC4WD) or the South District/Waterpocket District.

Several Days

Combine several day trip options.

Hike the shorter trails and routes in the South/Waterpocket District or North/Cathedral Valley.

Enjoy the park's pristine night sky by stargazing. Night sky charts are available at the visitor center.

Backpack into remote areas of the park and experience solitude and quiet. Remember to check for current weather, road, and trail conditions at the visitor center and get a permit if you plan to stay overnight.

Surrounding Treasures

You might be curious to know if there are some hidden gems close to Capitol Reef. Of course there are! Here you find a list of the must-do and unexpected places you should absolutely visit.

- **Grand Staircase-Escalante National Monument:** This National Monument is an absolute must-do. Definitely a "less traveled" wonder. Hikes here take you into slot canyons, along rivers, and include petroglyphs and views of cliff dwellings. We walked along the river for miles and did not see a single soul—but the scenery was spectacular! If you want to go there, we suggest you stay at Yonder Escalante, which is open from March to October. The place provides deluxe or tiny cabins, camping areas with tents, cars, or RVs, and vintage Airstreams transformed into luxurious rooms. Grand Staircase is absolutely incredible but overshadowed by the more popular parks, which is a good thing if you are looking for privacy and solitude. Our favorite hikes there include Zebra Slot Canyon, the Petrified Forest, and Devils Garden.

- **Zion and Canyonlands National Parks:** If you feel like Capitol Reef is not enough to satisfy your hunger for adventure, you can visit Zion National Park or Canyonlands National Park. Zion is among the most popular parks in the USA and is known for its sandstone cliffs and spectacular narrow paths you can walk through. Canyonlands is closer to Capitol Reef and also worth it! There, you can admire how the Colorado River shaped the area over the millennia. Countless canyons and formed buttes are waiting for you.

- **Dead Horse State Park:** If you visit Canyonlands National Park, you might notice that there's another park close to you—Dead Horse State Park. We absolutely recommend you stop by. Marvel at the breathtaking views over the canyons and the Colorado River. In particular, we suggest you go there at sunset. Take a picnic dinner and prepare to be amazed! From Dead Horse State Park, you can also easily reach another famous national park in Utah: Arches, quite possibly our all-time favorite national park.

- **Goblin Valley State Park:** Goblin Valley derives its name from its incredible and magical formations, which truly look like goblins. When walking around the park, you'll feel like you're in another dimension—far away from Earth. It's absolutely one of the most fascinating hidden gems in Utah! It's also just one hour away from Capitol Reef.

Nearby Cities

- **Torrey:** It's just 15 minutes from the park and offers a lot for it's size. If you remember, many restaurants and accommodations discussed in this chapter are located in this city. For more information, you can visit the website www.visitutah.com.

- **Hanksville:** It's 45 minutes from the park and has become increasingly popular because of its stunning views and breathtaking landscapes. For more information, you can visit the website www.hanksvilleutah.com.

- **Bicknell, Lyman, and Loa:** These tiny towns are about 20 to 30 minutes from the park and perfect if you are looking for solitude. For more information, you can visit the website www.capitolreefcountry.com.

- **Green River:** It's one hour and a half from Capitol Reef but the best location if you also want to visit Moab. In addition, Green River is between three of the most amazing parks in Utah: Capitol Reef, Arches, and Canyonlands. If you want to visit all of them without moving every time, you can stay in Green River. For more information, you can visit the website www.visitutah.com.

- **Salina:** It's one of the largest cities close to Capitol Reef and it's one hour and a half from the national park. It provides everything you need and much more! For more information, you can visit the website www.salinacity.org.

- **Richfield:** It's the largest city near the park and the place where you'll probably arrive by bus or shuttle if you take the plane. There, you'll find hiking trails and have the opportunity to visit Mystic Hot Springs and Red Hill Hot Springs. For more information, you can visit the website www.visitutah.com.

- **Escalante:** If you want to visit Capitol Reef and Bryce Canyon, you can stay in Escalante, which is not very big but has everything you need. It also provides unique accommodations and lots of fun activities to do. If you go to Escalante, we're sure you'll fall in love. We certainly did. This town definitely stole our hearts. For more information, you can visit the website www.visitutah.com.

In this chapter, we discovered all the amenities and hidden gems of Capitol Reef and the surrounding areas. We learned the best times to visit are spring and fall and we gathered information about where to stay, eat, and taste a craft beer or bottle of wine. We looked at the many scenic overlooks, and activities we can do inside the park. We also found a list of some of the most amazing trails and suggested itineraries depending on the time we can spend in Capitol Reef. Finally, we discovered surrounding treasures and nearby cities we must absolutely visit. Another chapter is about to begin, and another national park we'll explore! Now, it's time to tour Voyageurs National Park, in Minnesota.

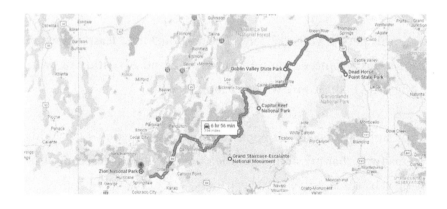

If you are finding this book helpful, please consider writing a "Review" for the Loneliest Treasures (and surrounding areas) - A US National Park Travel Guide by Beatrix & Zia!

National park enthusiasts, adventure seekers, hiking fans, and nature lovers around the world await your review.

People who give without expectation live longer, happier lives and make more money. So if we've got a shot at that during our time together, darn it, I'm gonna try.

To make that happen, I have a question for you...

Would you help someone you've never met, even if you never got credit for it?

Who is this person you ask? They are like you. Or, at least, like you used to be. Less experienced, wanting to have a grand adventure or two, and needing help, but not sure where to look.

Our mission is to make this book accessible to everyone. Everything we do stems from that mission. And, the only way for us to accomplish that mission is by reaching...well...everyone.

This is where you come in. Most people do, in fact, judge a book by its cover, and it's reviews. So here's my ask on behalf of a struggling national park lover you've never met:

Please help that person by leaving this book a review.

Your gift costs no money and less than 60 seconds to make real, but can change a fellow nature lovers life forever. Your review could help...

...one more small business provide for their community.
...one more entrepreneur support their family.
...one more employee get meaningful work.
...one more dream come true.

To get that 'feel good' feeling and help this person for real, all you have to do is...and it takes less than 60 seconds... leave a review.

Simply scan the QR code below to leave your review:

I'm that much more excited to help you enjoy a successful and enjoyable trip to the destinations of your choice than you can possibly imagine! You'll love the information I'm about to share in the coming chapters.
Thank you from the bottom of my heart. Now, back to our regularly scheduled programming.

- Your biggest fan, Beatrix Zia

PS - Fun fact: If you provide something of value to another person, it makes you more valuable to them. If you'd like goodwill straight from another national park enthusiast - and you believe this book will help them - send this book their way!

CHAPTER FOUR:
VOYAGEURS NATIONAL PARK
& SURROUNDING TREASURES,
MINNESOTA

My wish is to stay always like this, living quietly in a corner of nature. -Claude
Monet

Voyageurs National Park, located in Minnesota, comprises more than 200,000 acres and is one of the most remote and wildest parks in the USA (Pattiz, 2023f). This park is known for its spectacular hiking trails, interconnected waterways, and numerous historic sites. The name of the park comes from the French word *voyageurs*, which means "travelers," and was used to identify the French-Canadian fur traders who would pass through this area during the 18th and 19th centuries (Pattiz, 2023f).

This is the place where the water meets the woods, and that is what makes this park so special and unique. This park is absolutely for the adventurous at heart. This is the perfect place if you are looking for serenity and a way to escape! Beatrix and Zia are both in full agreement that one of the most exceptional things about this park (among many) is the nighttime sky.

The most fascinating aspect of Voyageurs is that it is predominantly water based. We went in October when the fall colors were at their most magnificent. This is also the best time if you are looking to experience the northern lights. This was a huge bucket list item for both of us and we were NOT disappointed. This is also the place where we first experienced the utter peacefulness of canoeing in remote lakes—definitely a favorite new pastime for us both. Let's just say—we will be returning.

Basic Information

Location

360 Hwy 11 East International Falls, MN 56649.

Entrance Passes

One of the great advantages of visiting this park is that it's completely free all year. You don't have to buy a pass or pay an entrance fee to visit Voyageurs (*Basic Information - Voyageurs National Park*, 2021).

Operating Hours and Seasons

Voyageurs National Park is open all year round and has three visitor centers: Rainy Lake, Kabetogama Lake, and Ash River. Rainy Lake is open all year but is closed during the week in fall and winter. The only days when it's open are Saturday and Sunday. Kabetogama Lake and Ash River are only open during summer, from May to September. For more information about the visitor centers and to check operating hours before arriving at the park, you can call (218) 286-5258 (*Basic Information - Voyageurs National Park*, 2021).

Best Times to Visit

There's no doubt about when you should visit the park: Fall. When September comes, the busy tourist season has come to an end and the area is much quieter and relaxing. The abundant tree foliage paints the park in red, yellow, and orange; the clear waters of the calm lakes reflect sunrises and sunsets; and the northern lights brighten up the night. There's no other way to describe fall in Voyageurs except for unforgettable! The main problem with visiting the park in fall is that you don't have much time, as the season is incredibly short in this area of the country. Starting from late September or early October, temperatures might begin to drop fast. In September, temperatures range between 66 °F and 48 °F and in October, it drops to between 49 °F and 37 °F (Lokvenec, 2023a). As you can see, temperatures can significantly change in just a couple of days or weeks.

For the above reason, we don't recommend you visit the park in winter, as temperatures drop as low as -55 °F (Pattiz, 2023a). We suggest you visit the park in winter only if you're an expert hiker and have the appropriate equipment to protect yourself from cold. Summer is the busiest season because the weather is pleasant and sunny days are longer and more frequent. However, the fact that the park has numerous lakes means that mosquitoes and flies are very common. If you visit during summer, make sure to bring repellent with you and dress accordingly. Spring is still a cold season, so there aren't many crowds or traffic.

How to Get There

Car

To reach Voyageurs National Park, you can drive from Minneapolis. The route is 280 miles long, lasts about 4 hour and a half hours, and is pleasant thanks to the evergreen trees that line the route. To reach the national park from Minneapolis, you must head north on Interstate 35 towards Forest Lake and Wyoming until you reach Cloquet. Exit there and take MN-33N. In Saginaw, turn left onto US Highway 53 N and follow the road until Voyageurs National Park. To save money, you can use your own car. If you want to rent one, we suggest you do it in Minneapolis, as you won't find other big cities along the way to the park. Alternatively, you can rent a car on the Turo app or www.outdoorsy.com where you'll have plenty of choice among cars, RVs, and other types of vehicles.

Plane

The fastest way to reach the park is obviously by plane, although this option is more expensive than renting a car and driving. The closest airport is Falls International Airport, only 45 minutes away from the park. To reach it, you can take a flight from Minneapolis St. Paul International Airport, which is about one and a half hours from Falls International Airport. You'll have the opportunity to rent a car at both airports.

Accommodations

You can find plenty of accommodation inside Voyageurs or nearby cities, especially in International Falls, which also provides the closest airport to the park.

- **Aspen Resort:** It provides rooms and a campground, a hot tub and heated pool, and fun activities for families and friends. It's open from May to October. For more information, you can call (218) 757-0098.

- **Frontier Resort:** It's been family-run for decades and provides cabins and campsites. To reach Voyageurs, you can rent a boat. It's open from May to October. For more information, you can call (218) 374-3311.

- **Northern Lights Resort:** It's located on the shores of Lake Kabetogama, right in the center of the park. You can rent a cabin or boat and come with a friend, although pets are allowed only in some cabins. It's open from May to October. For more information, you can call 800-318-7023.

- **Pine Point Lodge, Resort & Motel:** It's located on the shoreline of the park and has cottages. It's open from spring to fall. For more information, you can call 800-628-4446.

- **Pine Tree Cove Resort:** It's a family-run resort located on the west side of Lake Kabetogama that provides five comfortable cabins with everything you need. It's open from May to September. For more information, you can call (218) 875-2088.

- **The Voyageurs Motel:** It's located in International Falls and it's a cheap alternative to sleeping inside the park. It's eclectic and the staff are friendly. For more information, you can call (218) 283-9424.

- **Cantilever Hotel:** A few miles from International Falls, you find one of the best hotels of the area—Cantilever Hotel. It's a boutique hotel with its own distillery and restaurant. For more information, you can call (218) 540-1932.

- **Hilltop Lodge & Cabins:** It's located in International Falls, was built in the 1940s and has been recently renovated. It's absolutely one of the tourists' favorites in the area. It's comfortable and pet-friendly. For more information, you can call (218) 212-3315.

- **Camping:** If you plan to camp inside the park, you must know it's water-based so you will probably need a watercraft to reach camping sites. Moreover, lakes usually freeze between November and April or even May, so make sure to check weather conditions before going. If you have your own watercraft, you can go front country camping in one of the 137 sites spread across the park. Alternatively, there are two hike-in, primitive campsites and some remote areas where you can camp. For specific information, you can check the website www.nps. gov. You can also find campgrounds near the park, like Kabetogama Lake, Ash River Lake, Rainy Lake, and Crane Lake.

Remember you can always check Airbnb and Vrbo for more accommodations.

Restaurants

You'll only find one place where you can grab a bite inside the park, but you can choose among plenty of restaurants nearby.

- **Kettle Falls Hotel:** It's the only restaurant inside the park and remotely located at 15 miles from the nearest road. It's only accessible by watercraft and open from May to September. For more information, you can call (218) 240-1724 or (218) 240-1726.

- **Cantilever Distillery and Hotel:** If you have a passion for cocktails, you must have dinner there! It's located at International Falls and has been voted Best Cocktail Lounge and Distillery for two years in a row, so you won't be disappointed. For more information, you can call (218) 540-1932.

- **Coffee Landing Cafe:** It's located at International Falls and it's open for breakfast and lunch. The restaurant also provides brunch and vegetarian and vegan options. For more information, you can call (218) 373-2233.

- **Boston Pizza:** It's located at Fort Frances and provides an extensive menu with more than 100 items. As you might guess, the main meals include pizza, pasta, and burgers. For more information, you can call (807) 274-2727.

- **Montana Cafe:** It's located at Cook and famous for its excellent meals. It provides traditional American breakfast, brunch, and lunch. For more information, you can call (218) 666-2074.

- **Pattenn T Cafe:** It's located at Orr and is a typical family-run American restaurant. You can have breakfast or lunch there. For more information, you can call (218) 757-3908.

Gas Stations

There are no gas stations within Voyageurs, so make sure you fill the tank before getting there.

Shops, Groceries, or Markets Nearby

Inside the park, you'll find three bookstores managed by the non-profit association, *Jefferson National Parks Association* at the three visitor centers. Alternatively, there are many shops nearby.

- **International Mall Shopping Center:** It's a shopping center located at International Falls. As you might guess, you can find everything you need there. For more information, you can call (218) 283-9888.

- **Northwoods Gallery & Gifts:** It's located at Fort Frances and provides home decor and gift shops. If you want to find a nice present but don't know what to buy, you can try Northwood Gallery & Gifts!

For more information, you can call (807) 274-9224.

- **Border Bob's:** It's a nice art gallery in International Falls with lots of cool souvenirs. For more information, you can call (218) 283-4414.

- **Ronnings:** It's in International Falls and provides nice souvenirs. For more information, you can call (218) 283-8877.

- **Spirit of the Wilderness:** It's located at Saint Ely and if you need any sort of outdoor gear, you'll find what you're looking for there! For more information, you can call (218) 365-3149.

Breweries and Wineries

Are you looking for a relaxing place where you can enjoy some good beer or a glass of excellent wine after canoeing the waterways? You can choose among the wineries and breweries listed below.

- **Minneapolis Town Hall Brewery:** Located at 1430 Washington Ave S, Minneapolis.

- **Headflyer Brewing:** Located at 861 E. Hennepin Ave, Minneapolis.

- **Lakes & Legends Brewing Company:** Located at 1368 Lasalle Ave, Minneapolis.

- **Beaver Island Brewing Company:** Located at 216 6th Ave S, St. Cloud.

- **Morgan Creek Vineyards and Winery:** Located at 23707 478th Ave, New Ulm.

- **Grape Mill Vineyard and Winery:** Located at 18696 430th Ave SW,

East Grand Forks.

- **Whispering Oaks Winery and Black Oak Vineyard:** Located at 33578 Co Rd 30, Melrose.

- **L'Etoile Du Nord Vineyard LLC:** Located at 16451 NW Irene Court NE, Parkers Prairie.

Rules and Regulations

To preserve the environment, you can't use your own watercraft but only public boats, aircraft landings aren't authorized, and you can only use artificial bait if you want to fish in the lakes of the park. Pets aren't allowed on trails, except the Rainy Lake Recreation Trail, and in the back country. However, they're allowed on a leash in areas such as the visitor centers, campsites, and picnic areas. Hunting is not allowed. For more information about rules and regulations in Voyageurs National Park, you can visit www.nps.gov.

History and Trivia

Although French-Canadian fur traders started visiting the area in the 18th century, this doesn't mean nobody inhabited it before. In fact, the first people who occupied these lands arrived there around 10,000 years ago (Pattiz, 2023f). The main reason why the first tribes decided to establish themselves in Voyageurs National Park was the water, as fishing was a major source of food. You can still get a glimpse of the ancient inhabitants' lifestyle in the archaeological sites of the park (Pattiz, 2023f).

The most fascinating aspect of Voyageurs National Park is that is water-based (Pattiz, 2023f). We already mentioned water many times in this chapter, but never truly discussed how the park is organized. It contains more than 80,000 acres of water and more than 500 islands. The four largest lakes are Kabetogama, Rainy, Sand Point, and Namakan. If you want to visit the park, prepare to take a boat or another "watery" vehicle as that's the predominant way to tour the area (Pattiz, 2023f).

Things to Do in the Park

Let's take a look at the most interesting things you can do in Voyageurs National Park.

- **Admire the Ellsworth Rock Garden:** The Ellsworth Rock Garden is the result of one man's determination to build a terraced garden featuring original and spectacular artwork over a 20-year period. He started working in the 1940s and used monoliths to create unique pieces of art. It's just magnificent!

- **Enjoy the view at Junction Bay Falls:** The waterfalls of Namakan Lake are just breathtaking. They're perfect for sightseeing and quite picturesque.

- **Spot the park's wildlife:** The best place in the park to spot wildlife is Golden Portage, close to the Rainy Lake. From that point, you might see bald eagles, wolves, bears, moose, black ducks, and many more animals.

- **See the Grassy Bay Cliffs:** It's a 125-foot-high cliff over Sand Point Lake that is particularly beautiful during fall. From there, you can take stunning pictures of the park.

- **Fishing:** You can't avoid going fishing in a water-based park. The clear waters are perfect to catch a northern pike, muskie, or walleye. The best spots are Anderson Bay, Hoist Bay, Grassy Bay Cliffs, and Camp Marston.

- **Boat tours:** They usually start at Kabetogama Lake and Rainy Lake and can last from one hour and a half to more than six. In this way, you can enjoy the main amenities of the park while listening to a guide explaining everything.

- **Canoeing and cruising:** These are just two of the many watery activities you can try in the park.

- **Watch the sunset at Kabetogama Lake:** It's one of the most spectacular and terrific sunsets of all U.S. national parks! This is absolutely a must.

- **See the northern lights:** You might see northern lights anytime you go to Voyageurs, but you're more likely to spot them during fall and winter.

- **Enjoy the winter activities:** Visiting the park during winter means that it's very cold, but you can still try many things, like ice fishing, snowshoeing, skiing, and sledding.

Hiking Trails

Like in all national parks, you have plenty of opportunities to take a walk through beautiful settings. You will find some of the most scenic hiking trails below, from the easiest to the most difficult one.

- **Sullivan Bay Trail:** It's an easy hike that lasts about one hour and leads to a stunning viewpoint on Sullivan Bay.

- **Rainy Lake Recreation Trail:** It's an easy, paved trail that lasts between one and two hours that provides a peaceful experience.

- **Voyageurs Forest Overlook Trail:** It's an easy, short hike that lasts less than 30 minutes and allows you to walk through an amazing forest.

- **Kabetogama Lake Overlook Trail:** It's an easy, short hike that lasts between 10 and 30 minutes and leads you to an intimate spot where you can sit on a bench that overlooks the lake.

- **Echo Bay Trail:** This is a moderate hike that lasts between one and two hours. You will pass through rocky outcrops and lowlands. It's the perfect spot for some birdwatching! You might even spot a woodpecker.

- **Blind Ash Bay Trail:** It's a moderate, winding, and narrow trail that can last up to three hours, but it's absolutely worth it. You might not only get a glimpse of wild animals but can also take postcard pictures of Kabetogama Lake.

Surrounding Treasures

A surrounding treasure you shouldn't miss while visiting Voyageurs National Park is Isle Royale National Park, in Michigan. It's an isolated island that offers opportunities for all the adventurers out there! It's rugged and far from all other cities, places, and communities. To get there, you must cross Lake Superior by taking a ferry or a seaplane from Grand Portage or Grand Marais, in Minnesota. Go wild and explore Isle Royale National Park! You only live once.

Nearby Cities

You will find a list of the nearby cities worth visiting below.

- **International Falls:** Just 11 miles away from Voyageurs National Park, it's an amazing city that provides everything you need. As you've already found out throughout this chapter, International Falls has an airport and offers many places to sleep, eat, and shop. It's also a must for all nature lovers and hikers. For more information, you can visit the website www.exploreminnesota.com.

- **Kabetogama:** A community part of Kabetogama Township, in Saint Louis County. The community is located on the shores of the famous and spectacular Lake Kabetogama. For more information, you can visit the website www.exploreminnesota.com.

- **Crane Lake:** It's another community part of Crane Lake Township, in Saint Louis County. Crane Lake is the southern entrance to Voyageurs National Park and forms a large chain of lakes with Sand Point, Namakan, Ash River, and Kabetogama. For more information, you can visit the website www.visitcranelake.com.

In this chapter, we discovered almost everything about Voyageurs National Park. What distinguishes it from all other national parks is that it is water-based and you'll probably need a boat or another "watery" vehicle to visit it! The best time to go to Voyageurs is fall when foliage paints the park red, yellow, and orange. We also found that Kettle Falls Hotel is the only place inside the park where we can get a snack or meal and that there are no gas stations. Therefore, make sure to plan your trip and consider eating in one of the nearby cities, pack a picnic or two, or stock up on groceries if you want to camp within the park. We also looked at the most fascinating things to do in Voyageurs, which include hiking, seeing the breathtaking northern lights, watching wildlife, and enjoying a variety of water activities. Let's keep traveling and visit North Cascades National Park, in Washington.

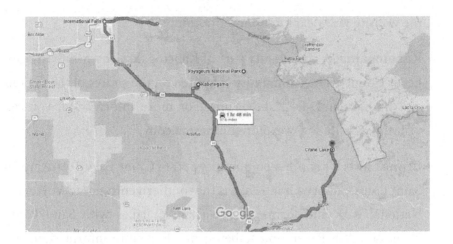

CHAPTER FIVE:
NORTH CASCADES NATIONAL
PARK & SURROUNDING TREASURES,
WASHINGTON

Nature always wears the colors of the spirit. -Ralph Waldo Emerson

North Cascades National Park is located in Washington and has the largest concentration of glaciers in the USA (Pattiz, 2023h). The park covers a bit more than 500,000 acres and was established in 1968. This beautiful place distinguishes itself in that it comprises more species than any other U.S. national park and is home to some endangered and threatened animals that can rarely be found in other areas of the state of Washington (Pattiz, 2023h).

We, Beatrix and Zia, found visiting North Cascades National Park to be a dreamy and surreal experience! It was part of our main summer trip one year. We booked a cabin there and also spent four days in nearby Olympic National Park—the two parks together were the perfect one-week vacation. The Blue Lake Trail in North Cascades was a favorite of ours! Absolutely beautiful, it was short (4.4 miles and easy to navigate), so that made it the perfect hike for us as one of our main excursions one day. The remaining trails are no less remarkable, but if done as a loop can be quite lengthy (6 miles or more). When hiking, our suggestion is to do an "out and back," which means to go out as far as you feel like, maybe 2.5 miles or so, depending on difficulty, and then head back.

Basic Information

Location

810 State Route 20 Sedro-Woolley, WA 98284.

Entrance Passes

North Cascades National Park is completely free, so you never have to pay an entrance fee or get a pass (Basic Information - North Cascades National

Park, 2022).

Operating Hours and Seasons

The park is open all year, every day. However, the operational season starts in May and ends in September. This means that some services are limited between October and April, including the visitor centers. The park has two visitor centers: North Cascade and Golden West. They both feature a bookstore, an information desk, exhibits, maps of the area, and ranger programs, and they're closed from October to April. For more information and to know the exact closure days of each visitor center, you can call (360) 854-7200 (Basic Information - North Cascades National Park, 2022).

Best Times to Visit

The best time to visit North Cascades is between mid-June to mid-September, as the weather is warmer and you're less likely to find snow on the hiking trails, except in the highest ones. As you might guess, summer is the busiest season, although the park is getting crowded in spring and fall, too. During that period, you're more likely to spot wildlife and the fall foliage is lovely. In addition, you must never forget you're at a high elevation where weather might change rapidly. In fact, storms are common, so you must be prepared to face rain and wind during your stay. Avalanches are also frequent and every winter brings heavy rain and snow to the park. If you plan to visit North Cascades during summer, you might want to know that the east side is always drier and warmer, as temperatures reach 90° F, so you might prefer to visit that area instead of the west side (Weather - North Cascades National Park, 2017).

How to Get There

Car

To reach North Cascades National Park, you'll have to drive through State Route 20 or North Cascades Highway, to take you to different areas of the park.

- **North Cascades Highway:** If you arrive from the west, you can take Interstate 5 and reach Exit 230 at Burlington where you enter State Route 20 or North Cascades Highway. If you arrive via State Route 20 from the east, you take U.S. Route 97 at Okanogan or State Route 153 at Twisp. Make sure to check weather and road conditions, as some routes might be closed due to avalanche danger and often during the entire winter season, sometimes starting as early as November.

- **Mount Shuksan and Copper Ridge:** If you're a hiker or climber and want to rapidly access Mount Shuksan and Copper Ridge, you can take State Route 542 east of Bellingham.

- **Hozomeen:** The only way to access the Ross Lake shoreline is through the Silver-Skagit road to Hozomeen.

Plane

- **Seattle-Tacoma International Airport:** It's about 120 miles from the North Cascades visitor center and the nearest major airport.

- **Chelan Seaplanes:** It offers floatplane access from the city of Chelan to Stehekin and Lake Chelan National Recreation Area.

- **Vancouver International Airport:** It's approximately 130 miles from the North Cascades visitor center and 135 miles from Hozomeen.

- **Pangborn Memorial Airport:** It offers limited flights to Wenatchee and Chelan.

- **Bellingham International Airport:** It offers limited flights to Northwest Washington.

You can also rent a car or an RV at the airports. If you're looking for something different and more affordable, remember you can always check the Turo app to rent a vehicle from a local! If you're looking to rent a campervan or RV, you can also visit the websites www.cruiseamerica.com or www.outdoorsy.com, as mentioned in previous chapters. *Escape Rentals U.S.A.* is perfect for affordable rentals while *Campervan North America* has a wide selection of campervans. Both companies are located in Seattle. To contact *Escape Rentals U.S.A.* you can call (877) 270-8267 while to contact *Campervan North America*, call (208) 712-8100.

Accommodations

There are various options available to you for sleeping inside or out at North Cascades National Park, but we decided to just include three of them in the list below. They're the top three accommodations in the area and are all perfect for individuals, couples, or groups! At the end of the list, you'll also find camping options.

- **North Cascades Lodge at Stehekin:** If you want to enjoy breathtaking views from your windows when you wake up in the morning, this is the place. The lodge provides comfortable and rustic rooms on the shore of Lake Chelan, a restaurant, and a gift shop.

The staff also organize activities like horseback riding, kayaking, and fishing. However, you'll have to sweat to reach the lodge! To get there, you have two possibilities: Take the ferry or enjoy an amazing 23-mile hike from Highway 20 to High Bridge where you'll find the bus that takes you to Stehekin. To make a reservation, you can call (855) 685-4167 or (509) 699-2056.

- **Stehekin Valley Ranch:** Located nine miles from Lake Chelan, it's perfect if you prefer staying in a more isolated area and relaxing in nature. The ranch offers tent and ranch cabins, wagons, or the Ranch House for families or small groups. The Cookhouse provides all sorts of meals for guests. There are also a variety of on-site recreational options, like the reading room, or outdoor areas to play badminton, ping pong, croquet, and much more! The ranch also offers activities, like kayaking or horseback riding. Stehekin Valley Ranch can't be reached by car, so you'll have to take a boat, airplane, or hike. For more information, you can call (509) 682-4677.

- **Ross Lake Resort:** You can stay at the resort or camp overnight and enjoy the spectacular view from Ross Lake. To get there, you can take the Diablo Ferry or hike for a mile and take a quick shuttle ride through to the lake. Just be aware there's no restaurant or store inside the resort, so plan accordingly. For more information, you can call (206) 486-3751.

- **Campgrounds:** You have plenty of opportunities to camp inside North Cascades. Among the main campgrounds, you'll find Gorge Lake, Newhalem Creek, Colonial Creek North, Colonial Creek South, Goddell Creek, and Lower Goddell Creek.

Remember you can always check Airbnb and VRBO for more accommodations in the area. If you check Airbnb and look for unconventional options, we highly recommend you take a look at **North Cascades Haven at the River Cabin**, in Marblemount. You can rent an entire cabin with a balcony that overlooks the Cascade River. It's the perfect place to take some time for yourself and just relish the gorgeous views. You can also find it on Instagram: *north_cascades_haven*.

Restaurants

Inside the park, North Cascades Lodge at Stehekin is the only place where you'll be able to eat. Therefore, make sure to plan your trip accordingly and consider bringing food with you. Alternatively, you can have a meal at one of the restaurants below.

- **Stehekin Pastry Company:** It's in the vicinity of the docking area in Stehekin and provides delicious breakfasts, lunches, and brunches with vegan options. For more information, you can call (509) 682-7742.

- **Sun Mountain Lodge:** It's a resort in Winthrop that provides a bar and lounge area. The reason why we recommend it is because it has the most spectacular views in the whole state of Washington! For more information, you can call (509) 383-8011.

- **Heather Meadows Cafe:** If you're looking for an affordable and delicious option for lunch, you can go to Heather Meadows Cafe, in Glacier. For more information, you can call (360) 734-6771.

- **Up River Grill & Tavern:** Located in Marblemount, it provides tasty lunches and dinners at reasonable prices. It also has a patio that allows you to eat while looking at nature around you. For more information, you can call (360) 873-4221.

- **Marblemount Diner:** It's one of the few alternatives to Up River Grill & Restaurant in Marblemount and a bit more expensive. It's famous for its delicious burgers and pies. For more information, you can call (360) 873-4503.

- **Mondo Restaurant:** Located in Marblemount, it provides American and Asian food at reasonable prices. It also has vegetarian and gluten-free options and it's open for breakfast, lunch, and dinner. For more information, you can call (360) 873-2111.

- **The Eatery:** Located in Rockport, it provides breakfast, lunch, and dinner at reasonable prices. For more information, you can call (360) 873-2414.

Shops, Groceries, or Markets Nearby

You can find many shops and grocery stores close to North Cascades National Park.

- **Mazama Store:** It provides a good selection of food and is famous for its bakery and coffee. The address is 50 Lost River Rd, Mazama. For more information, you can call (509) 996-2855.

- **Hank's Market:** It's a small, family-owned grocery store that has everything you need. The address is 412 E Methow Valley Hwy, Twisp. For more information, you can call (509) 997-7711.

- **Evergreen IGA:** It provides a solid selection of locally-produced goods at reasonable prices. It's not like any other IGA! The address is 920 Hwy 20, Winthrop. For more information, you can call (509) 996-2525.

- **Tenderfoot:** It's a lesser-known grocery store with a good selection and affordable prices. It also provides souvenirs and art supplies. The address is 177 Riverside Ave, Winthrop. For more information, you can call (509) 996-2288.

- **Glover Street Market:** It's a grocery store with a self-serve bar where you can eat breakfast or lunch. Service and food are both good. The address is 124 Glover St N, Twisp. For more information, you can call (509) 997-1320.

- **Manson Red Apple Market:** It provides a grocery store, meat shop, and gas station. It might be a bit more expensive than other markets, but worth it! It provides a great variety of food and tasty wines and beers. The address is 610 E Wapato Way, Manson. For more information, you can call (509) 687-9333.

- **The Carlton General Store:** It provides a gas station and grocery store and has everything you need. The address is 2256 State Rte 153, Carlton. For more information, you can call (509) 997-9022.

Breweries and Wineries

Now, let's look at some of the best breweries and wineries you can find near North Cascades National Park. It can be so good to relax in front of a tasty glass of wine or beer at the end of a long but exciting day in nature.

- **Roslyn Brewing Company:** Located at 208 W Pennsylvania Ave,

Roslyn.

- **Silver Lake Winery:** Located at 1500 Vintage Rd, Zillah.

- **Iron Horse Brewery:** Located at 416 N Main St, Ellensburg.

- **Treveri Cellars:** Located at 71 Gangl Rd, Wapato.

- **Swiftwater Cellars:** Located at 301 Rope Rider Dr, Cle Elum.

- **Pyramid Brewery and Alehouse:** Located at 1201 1st Ave S, Seattle.

Rules and Regulations

If you plan to visit North Cascade with your pet, you must check rules and regulations first. In fact, pets aren't allowed inside the park except with a leash on the Pacific Crest Trail, Ross Lake, Chelan Lake National Recreation Areas, and surrounding national forest lands. For more detailed information, you can visit the website www.nps.gov.

History and Trivia

Let's find out more about the peculiarities of North Cascades. First of all, the park is actually a complex because it's divided into North Cascades National Park, Ross Lake National Recreation Area, and Chelan Lake Recreation Area, which includes Stehekin (Julie, 2020). There's only one road inside the park which is referred to as Highway 20 or North Cascades Highway.

Why is this park special? It contains more than 300 glaciers and 300 lakes, which is the largest glacial system in the entire USA other than Alaska (Julie, 2020). Most of the mountains are more than 8,000 feet. A fun fact about the park is the "fun" names some mountains were given. A few of them include Ghost Peak, Mount Terror, and Phantom Peak. Despite its unmatched beauty, North Cascades is one of the least visited national parks in the USA (Julie, 2020). If you want to be sure not to meet crowds and get stuck in traffic, this is the place.

Things to Do in the Park

As there are many lakes in the park, things to do mainly include water activities. Motor boating, kayaking, and canoeing are some of the most popular practices in North Cascades. The best places to try such activities are Lake Ross, Chelan, Gorge, and Diablo. If you want to rent a boat, you must go to the Ross Lake Resort. If you want, you can also try boat camping in Lake Ross and Chelan. However, you would need a permit to do so. Personal watercraft aren't allowed and water sports like tubing or waterskiing are prohibited. During the summer season, you can also try kayaking and rafting at Skagit River and Stehekin River.

Hiking Trails

Hiking trails at North Cascades are just amazing! You can choose among a number of easy and moderate trails, all with stunning views over the park.

- **Gorge Creek Falls Loop:** It's an easy loop of 0.5 miles that requires between 15 and 20 minutes. The trail is flat and provides scenic views over the park.

- **Trail of the Cedars:** It's an accessible round-trip hike of 0.3 miles. It requires about 20 to 30 minutes and is suitable for everyone! The most spectacular part of this trail is the beginning where you walk across a suspension bridge over Skagit River.

- **Sterling Munro Boardwalk Trail:** It's an easy 0.3-mile round trip that takes less than 20 minutes. This is the perfect trail if you are looking for a place to take stunning pictures and enjoy the scenic overlooks over the mountains.

- **Ladder Creek Falls Trail:** It's an easy 0.5-mile round trip that takes about 30 minutes. This trail is absolutely amazing as it allows you to walk over cool bridges and boardwalks that lead you to a breathtaking waterfall. This trail is amazing from the beginning to the end.

- **Blue Lake Trail:** It's a moderate 4.6-mile trail that requires about 3 hours. It's one of the best hikes in North Cascades, as it not only provides spectacular views of the park but also jaw-dropping sights of the Cascades. Although it's considered a moderate hike, it's not too hard, so you might give it a try even if you're not an avid hiker.

- **Diablo Lake Trail:** It's a moderate 7.5-mile hike that requires between 3.5 and 4.5 hours, so you must have some experience if you want to try it. The effort is absolutely worth it as this is one of the most famous hikes in the park! If you've ever imagined North Cascades as a place full of blue, crystal-clear lakes surrounded by mountains or saw some pictures that showed similar scenery, then you've imagined and seen Diablo Lake Trail. If you want to try it, start at the ferry terminal at the Ross Lake Resort and walk through to the Ross Lake Dam.

Surrounding Treasures

As already mentioned in the beginning of this chapter, a national park that is very close to North Cascades and absolutely worth a visit is Olympic

National Park. The two parks are only two hours away from each other, so they can make the perfect one-week vacation! If you plan to go on a road trip from North Cascades to Olympic National Park, there are some places you must stop by. You must visit Bellevue, Seattle, Tacoma, and Olympia, and see the Chain Lakes Loop Trailhead, Nooksack Falls, and the Big Four Ice Caves. These are just a few of the amazing things you can find along the way! Once you reach Olympic National Park, you won't be disappointed. You'll find a magnificent place that encompasses three different ecosystems: Old-growth temperate rain forest, glacier-capped mountains, and wild Pacific coast.

Nearby Cities

You won't find big cities close to North Cascades, but there are tiny gems that are absolutely worth a visit!

- **Marblemount:** This little town is located very close to Skagit River and is considered a hidden gem. It's halfway between North Cascades and Wenatchee National Forest and the perfect place for activities like climbing, canoeing, hiking, and fishing. For more information, you can visit www.visitskagitvalley.com.

- **Winthrop:** It's a small, old western town that provides everything you need. Here, you'll find restaurants, boutiques, affordable and luxurious accommodations, and antique boardwalks. It also provides plenty of outdoor activities and is just a step away from Okanogan National Forest. For more information, you can visit www. winthropwashington.com.

- **Mazama:** Located in the Methow Valley, it offers lots of activities in winter and summer, like horseback riding, hiking, skiing, and mountain biking. For more information, you can visit www.scenicwa. com.

- **Concrete:** It's a small town located near the entrance of North Cascades and characterized by historic buildings and landmarks. It's surrounded by mountains and lakes that provide plenty of opportunities to try activities like fishing, hiking, kayaking, and much more. For more information, you can visit www.concrete-wa.com.

In this chapter, we discovered everything we need to know about North Cascades National Park. Even if it's one of the least visited parks in the USA, it's a real treasure! With all its glaciers and lakes, you'll be amazed at the stunning views and hiking trails. In addition, you'll enjoy plenty of water activities, like kayaking or canoeing. Near North Cascades, you can visit Olympic National Park and some of the small towns that surround the park, like Marblemount and Winthrop. If you plan to visit this area, we suggest you go between mid-June and mid-September when the climate is perfect. Now, it's time to continue our journey and visit Guadalupe Mountains National Park.

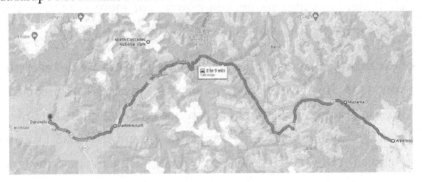

CHAPTER SIX:
GUADALUPE MOUNTAINS NATIONAL PARK & SURROUNDING TREASURES, TEXAS

The mountains are calling and I must go. -John Muir

Guadalupe Mountains National Park is located in Texas and comprises more than 86,000 acres (Pattiz, 2023b). The most astonishing thing about this park is that it includes the highest peak in Texas, which is Guadalupe Peak, and reaches almost 9,000 feet of elevation! The national park was established in 1972 and the first known tribes to inhabit the area were the renowned Apaches, who consider the place a sanctuary. When the first settlers arrived, bloody conflicts began until the Apaches were forced to leave. Guadalupe Mountains National Park is also a special place because of the legends that surround it. Apparently, gold has always been found in the area and Apaches used to have it (Pattiz, 2023b).

When we, Beatrix and Zia, visited the park for the first time, the only word we could think of to describe it was "stunning." Imagine hiking trails through peaceful wooded areas, fascinating local history, and the world's largest and most extensive Permian Fossil Reef. The bright white Salt Basin Dunes and the grasslands literally teeming with wildlife were just a couple of our favorite things about this remote treasure. Let's find out more about this park.

Basic Information

Location

400 Pine Canyon, Salt Flat, TX 79847.

Entrance Passes

To visit Guadalupe Mountains, you must pay an entrance fee of $10.00. Alternatively, you can buy the annual pass at $35.00 that allows you to tour the park whenever you want within one year from the moment you get the pass (*Basic Information - Guadalupe Mountains National Park*, 2023). The interagency passes discussed in Chapter 1 are also valid.

Operating Hours and Seasons

Guadalupe Mountains National Park is divided into five districts: Pine Springs, Dog Canyon, Frijole Ranch, Salt Basin Dunes, and McKittrick Canyon (*Basic Information - Guadalupe National Park*, 2023). Pine Springs and Dog Canyon are open all day, every day except during holidays. Frijole Ranch and Salt Basin Dunes are open every day from sunrise to 30 minutes after sunset except during holidays. McKittrick Canyon is open every day from 8.00 a.m. to 5.00 p.m. except during holidays (*Basic Information - Guadalupe National Park*, 2023).

The park also has three visitor centers: Pine Springs, Dog Canyon, and McKittrick Canyon. Pine Springs is the main visitor center where you can pay fees, get maps and souvenirs, tour the museum, and obtain permits. Keep in mind you'll always need a permit for overnight stays and will have to pay a small fee. Pine Springs is open all day, every day, from 8.00 a.m. to 4.00 p.m. Dog Canyon is a ranger station that opens only when staff are available, so operating hours vary a lot. We suggest you call before going, to check the staff's availability. McKittrick Canyon is open all day, every day, from 8.00 a.m. to 5.00 p.m. (*Basic Information - Guadalupe National Park*, 2023).

For more information about the park districts and visitor centers, you can call (915) 828-3251.

Best Times to Visit

The best times to visit Guadalupe Mountains National Park are spring and fall when it's not too hot or cold to enjoy a walk and some time to relax in the solitude. In particular, we suggest you visit between mid-October and early November to see the maple leaves in McKittrick Canyon changing colors for the season. You'll be amazed by that unrivaled show in Texas! The main disadvantage of visiting Guadalupe Mountains during spring or fall is crowds and traffic. But don't be discouraged, as this park is one of the loneliest in the USA, apart from Alaska (Derr, 2014). Another little secret about Guadalupe Mountains is that it's located in the darkest corner of Texas, which means it's the best place to just lie down and stargaze at night! If you want to avoid crowds at the cost of missing the best period to visit the park, you can take a tour at the end of August. It's not as impressive as spring or fall, but still very much worth it.

How to Get There

Car

Guadalupe Mountains National Park is on the north side of US Highway 62/180. If you arrive from El Paso, you must drive for 110 miles east of the city to reach the Pine Springs visitor center. If you arrive from Van Horn, you must drive north on US 54 and turn right at US 62/180. If you arrive from Carlsbad, you must drive through US Highway 62/180 South. If you plan to arrive at Dog Canyon Visitor Center, you must drive through New Mexico State Road 137. Dog Canyon is a two-hour drive from Pine Springs.

Plane

If you want to arrive by plane, you'll probably need to get a flight to El Paso, then drive to Guadalupe Mountains. Alternatively, you might take a flight to either New Mexico, Lubbock, or Midland. Texas and Mesa Airlines also connect Albuquerque and Carlsbad. El Paso is the closest major airport to the park and it takes about one and a half hours to reach Guadalupe Mountains from there. The closest airport is in Carlsbad, which is only 30 minutes away from the park, but it's smaller than El Paso. If you take a flight to Midland, you'll have to drive for three hours to get to Guadalupe Mountains, but it's absolutely worth it! You'll have the opportunity to see some amazing landscapes along the way.

Bear in mind no public transportation or shuttle service is available in the park. If you arrive by plane, you'll need to drive to reach Guadalupe Mountains. If you want to rent a car or RV, you can do it at the airport or use the Turo app to rent from locals.

But what if you want to travel through the country by train or bus? If you take the train, you'll find an Amtrak station at El Paso, then you can drive or take a Greyhound to reach the park. In fact, El Paso is the closest Greyhound station that allows you to comfortably reach Guadalupe Mountains without having to drive yourself.

Accommodations

If you're planning a trip to the Guadalupe Mountains, you must know it's an isolated place. In fact, you won't find any lodging, hotels, or restaurants inside the park. Unfortunately, this means you'll have to stay in one of the nearby cities—unless you want to camp. The most recommended places to sleep when visiting Guadalupe Mountains are Carlsbad, Van Horn, and El Paso.

- **Carlsbad:** It's 55 miles from Pine Springs Visitor Center and is a lovely little city. There, you'll find many of the big hotel chains, so you won't have problems finding accommodations. Among them, we recommend you try Hyatt House, which is a modern hotel conveniently located off the US Highway 62. For more information about Hyatt House, you can call (575) 689-6700. In our opinion, Carlsbad is the best option for lodging.

- **Van Horn:** It's 64 miles away from the main park entrance and smaller than Carlsbad, so accommodation options are limited. We recommend you stay at El Capitan, a hotel full of history and nostalgia that provides a true Texas experience. For more information about El Capitan, you can call (432) 283-1220.

- **El Paso:** It's the biggest and most touristy city close to Guadalupe Mountains, so you might want to avoid it if you're looking for a place to stay away from crowds. At the same time, you'll find plenty of places to stay at night, from more affordable options to expensive hotels.

- **Campgrounds inside the park:** Guadalupe Mountains lacks in hotels but provides plenty of opportunities to camp! There are three developed campgrounds: Pine Springs, Dog Canyon, and Frijole Horse Corral. They are all accessible by car or RV and reservable up to six months in advance from www.recreation.gov. Pine Springs Campground is near the visitor center and provides potable water, restrooms, and utility sinks. Dog Canyon Campground has four RV sites and nine tent sites and is a bit more isolated than Pine Springs. Frijole Horse Corral Campground is just a mile away from Pine Springs visitor center and close to the highway. For more information about the campgrounds, you can visit www.nps.gov.

- **Campgrounds outside the park:** You can choose among a number of campgrounds outside the park. In the northeast, you will find Chosa Campground area and Sunset Reef Campground. If you have an RV, you can stay at White's City RV Park or Carlsbad RV Park. South of the park, you can try Van Horn RV Park or Southern Star RV Park.

As always, remember to check Airbnb and Vrbo or more accommodations!

Goods and Services

Your visit to Guadalupe Mountains National Park requires planning, as you won't find any grocery stores or restaurants inside the park. Therefore, you'll need to bring your own food. In general, services are extremely limited, so plan accordingly. You won't find any gas stations inside the park or within a 35-mile radius in either direction from Pine Springs visitor center. This means you'll have to bring gasoline with you or make sure you fill the tank before arriving at the park. You'll find gas stations in Van Horn and El Paso. If you travel from New Mexico, you'll find the last gas station at Withes City. As you also learned in the previous sections, developed campgrounds inside the park are basic. Make sure to consider all of the above factors before embarking on your journey to Guadalupe Mountains National Park.

Breweries and Wineries

As you might guess, finding a good winery or brewery close to Guadalupe Mountains National Park is not easy. You would need to go to one of the nearby cities, like Carlsbad, or even El Paso if you want to have more options. Let's look at some of the best breweries and wineries close to the park.

- **Guadalupe Mountains Brewing Company:** Located at 3324 National Parks Highway, Carlsbad.

- **La Vina Winery:** Located at 4201 South Highway NM-28, El Paso.

- **Sombra Antigua Vineyard and Winery:** Located at 430 La Vina Road, El Paso.

- **Blazing Tree Brewery:** Located at 11426 Rojas Dr Ste A-13, El Paso.

- **Mountain Star Brewing Company:** Located at 11135 Pellicano Dr., El Paso.

Rules and Regulations

You have to pay a fee to enter the park and get a permit if you plan to stay overnight. In addition, you must also consider rules about pets if you want to bring your fur friend with you. Pets must always be kept on a leash and are allowed only in areas that can be accessed by vehicles, like parking or picnic areas, and roadsides. Pets aren't allowed in public buildings, the backcountry, and all hiking trails except the one that goes from Pine Springs Campground to Pinery Trail.

History and Trivia

Guadalupe Mountains National Park is certainly renowned for its amazing wildlife. As the area is a desert, animals aren't easy to spot. They tend to hide during the day to avoid wandering in the hottest hours and prefer going out when the safety and comfort of night arrives. If you stay overnight, you might be lucky enough to see a coyote, bobcat, mountain lion, or badger in the distance. Early in the morning and late in the evening you might also spot black-tailed jackrabbits, mule deer, or javelinas.

Guadalupe Mountains National Park has also been home to a series of bloody conflicts between Native Americans and early settlers, as we already mentioned in the beginning. For centuries, the so-called Mescalero Apaches inhabited the area (Pattiz, 2023b). Their name derives from their frequent use of the agave plant, which is translated into "Mescal" in Spanish. From the mid-1860s, Mescalero Apaches started a conflict with the Buffalo Soldiers, who constituted the 10th cavalry regiment. Mescalero Apaches called those soldiers "Buffalo Soldiers" due to their dark and curly hair. Conflicts continued for years, until the Buffalo Soldiers managed to destroy all Apache camps, forcing them to leave the area. The Mescalero Apaches who survived the raids were brought to nearby reservations (Pattiz, 2023b).

Scenic Drives and Overlooks

Guadalupe Mountains National Park is so isolated that no roads pass through it. This means you won't be delighted by scenic overlooks from the comfort of your car. However, many routes lead to and provide access to the park. You'll find a list of the most spectacular viewpoints and roads outside of the park below.

- **Highway 62/180:** It's one of the most scenic drives in Texas and a must-see! It connects El Paso and Carlsbad and provides stunning mountain views all along the way. The route takes about four hours and is characterized by access roads that approach Guadalupe Mountains National Park.

- **El Capitan Viewpoint:** If you climb up Guadalupe Pass on Highway 62/180 for less than an hour, you will find a viewpoint with a spectacular view of El Capitan, a peak a bit less high than Guadalupe Peak.

- **Guadalupe Peak Viewpoint:** Southeast of the park boundary is the Guadalupe Peak Viewpoint where you can admire the magnificent Guadalupe Peak, the highest point in Texas. You can just pop a squat and enjoy nature!

- **Five Points Visa:** Near the end of the Guadalupe Rim Road, there's a scenic lookout called Five Points Vista, the perfect spot to look at the rim and the mountains in the distance.

- **Dog Canyon:** It's the park's remote north district and it's only seven miles from Pine Springs, although it takes about two hours to reach this stunning viewpoint. It's absolutely worth it!

- **Williams Ranch:** If you want to get off the beaten path and have a vehicle that can easily cross a primitive road, you must go to Williams Ranch! It offers a closer look at the typical western escarpment that characterizes Guadalupe Mountains.

- **Highway 54:** It's a two-hour drive that leads you from Van Horn to the park. While driving, you'll have the chance to look at the Delaware Mountains to the east and Sierra Diablo to the west.

- **Salt Basin Dunes:** It's a remote and lesser-known area that reminds you of the ancient origins of the park. Its dunes are a clear sign that the area was underwater millennia ago.

Things to Do in the Park

If you visit Guadalupe Mountains National Park, you must absolutely go during fall and enjoy some horseback riding. As we already mentioned when discussing the best times to visit the park, the landscapes completely transform and become almost magic during fall. That's because the leaves decorate the trails in a rainbow of colors! The best place to go to admire such stunning scenery is McKittrick Canyon. In particular, you can hike Devil's Hall or Smith Spring Trail to experience all the beauty and brilliance of the fall colors.

As mentioned above, another great activity within the park is horseback riding. However, you must bring your own horse with you. To experience this, you'll need to get the free Wilderness Use Permit at Pine Springs visitor center to report the route you want to take and how many people and animals will participate on the trip. Off-trail riding is not allowed and you can only go on certain trails. Easy trails are Foothill and Frijole, moderate are Marcus and Salt Basin Overlook, and strenuous are Teja and El Capitan. For more information on the allowed trails, you can visit www.nps.gov.

Hiking Trails

Obviously, there are many hiking trails in Guadalupe Mountains National

Park. You'll find a list of some of the most popular, easy and moderate trails below.

- **Pine Springs Campground Loop:** It's an incredibly short hike that only requires a few minutes and it's perfect for walking and camping. You'll likely find a lot of people depending on the time of year or maybe not—it's a lonely park after all.

- **The Pinery:** It's an easy hike that is less than a mile and takes about 20 minutes. It's a popular trail but you'll likely find some peace and solitude early in the morning or late in the evening.

- **Foothills Trail:** It's a 4-mile easy trail with a bit more elevation than the Pinery but still feasible for almost everyone. It's an out-and-back trail that requires about an hour and a half and is less popular than the Pinery. You'll probably spot some birds along the trail.

- **McKittrick Canyon Trail to Hunter Line Shack:** It's a 7-mile moderate hike that takes about two and a half hours to complete. It's also a popular trail, so you might find other hikers along the way.

- **El Capitan Trail:** It's a 9-mile moderate trail that's absolutely amazing! If you're an expert hiker or have some experience, we recommend you give it a try. It takes a bit more than four hours and provides stunning views of the park. It's also unlikely you'll meet other people.

- **Pratt Cabin via McKittrick Canyon Trail:** It's a 5-mile, out-and-back hike that requires less than two hours. It's likely you'll see some birds along the way.

Suggested Itineraries

You might wonder how you can take advantage of every single minute you spend in Guadalupe Mountains National Park, especially if you don't have a lot of time. We've thought about everything for you. Here you'll find suggested itineraries based on the amount of available time. Choose the one that best suits your timeframe.

One Hour

Stop by the Pine Springs visitor center, walk through the museum, and walk the Pinery Trail.

Half Day

Stretch your legs and take a scenic hike or two! In addition to the hikes listed in the previous section, you can also try the Smith Spring Trail, which is a 2.3-mile round trip, or the Devil's Hall Trail, which is a 4.3-mile round-trip.

Full Day

Pick a day hike that can take you into a riparian area or high up into the conifer forest. Common day hikes include the Guadalupe Peak Trail, the Bowl Trail, or the McKittrick Canyon Trail leading to the Grotto.

Surrounding Treasures

You might have already noticed that there's not much to see close to the park. Yet, this absolutely doesn't mean that you shouldn't visit Guadalupe Mountains National Park. One interesting fact about the park is that 95% of the area is officially designated "Wilderness," which means that facilities and improvements are provided only where they are necessary. In other words, campgrounds, trails, and signs are very limited (The Guadalupe Mountains Wilderness, 2022). This way, the wilderness of the park can be better preserved. Another area you must absolutely visit is the Frijole Ranch, which is considered an oasis on the Guadalupe escarpment. There, you will also find a museum that teaches you about the history of the park, from the first Native American tribes who lived there to more recent times. As you look around, you can imagine how life might have been centuries ago. For more information about the Guadalupe Mountains Wilderness and Frijole Ranch, you can visit the website www.nps.gov.

In this chapter, we took a trip to Guadalupe Mountains National Park, the Apaches' home for centuries. You discovered that the best time to visit is fall when the park is awash in brilliant golds, pinks, and reds! The best place to admire this scenery is McKittrick Canyon. You also learned you must travel to the park by car, even if you take the plane from a nearby city. But the most important thing you must remember is that there are very few facilities inside the park. No restaurants, accommodations, gas stations, or grocery stores can be found. This means you must carefully plan your trip and make sure you get everything you need before arriving in the park. The closest cities to obtain basic goods and find accommodations are Van Horn, Carlsbad, and Whites City. Alternatively, you can camp in one of the campgrounds inside Guadalupe Mountains to enjoy the wilderness and gaze at the stars that adorn the night sky! Now, it's time to continue our journey and discover everything about Great Basin National Park, in Nevada.

CHAPTER SEVEN: GREAT BASIN NATIONAL PARK & SURROUNDING TREASURES, NEVADA

Adopt the pace of nature: her secret is patience. -Ralph Waldo Emerson

Established in 1986, Great Basin National Park is located in Nevada and covers almost 80,000 acres (Pattiz, 2023d). The attraction that makes this park unique is the Lehman Caves, which are a series of underground passageways created by water erosion. While walking through those caves, you'll be amazed by all the stalactites and stalagmites that create an enchanting environment. Great Basin is also home to the highest peak in Nevada, Mount Wheeler, which is a bit more than 13,000 feet high.

Please be aware that this park can range from 6,000 feet to over 13,000 feet in elevation. Altitude sickness can be a very real concern if you are not acclimated. This can cause light headedness, racing heart, weakness and nausea, which can definitely affect your visit to the park and your activities while there, so please plan and prepare accordingly.

When we, Beatrix and Zia, visited the park, we were in wholehearted agreement: This landscape is not only beautifully rugged but shockingly picturesque as well—the perfect combo. Talk about being able to escape the crowds and find peace in an absolutely stunning place. You will drive the "Loneliest Road In America" to get there without seeing another car. One of the most enjoyable activities we did was undoubtedly the ranger-led hike to the Lehman Caves. How unique? A definite must-do. Some of the hikes we liked most were the Sky Islands Forest Trail, the Alpine Lakes Loop, and Bristlecone Trail. Between the three you get the perfect feel for the varying landscapes in this incredible park. A best-kept secret for sure.

Basic Information

Location

Lehman Caves Visitor Center, NV 488, Baker 89311.

Entrance Passes

One of the advantages of visiting Great Basin is that it's completely free. If you're interested, the staff inside the park sell America the Beautiful National Parks & Federal Recreational Lands Passes. If you want to try the Lehman Caves Tour, you must pay a fee which is not covered by the annual interagency passes discussed in Chapter 1. You'll have to pay a fee also for camping and for the RV sanitary station.

You'll have to make a reservation to camp in many campgrounds and to do the Lehman Caves tour. To reserve your place, visit the website www. recreation.gov. You'll also need to get a free backcountry permit to camp near Johnson or Baker Lakes, picnic in the Upper Lehman Group Picnic Area, and practice wild caving. For more information, you can visit the website www.nps.gov.

Operating Hours and Seasons

The park is open all year and has two visitor centers: Lehman Caves and Great Basin. They both provide restrooms, water, parking, exhibits, and give you the opportunity to watch the park movie. However, you can get tickets and permits only at Lehman Caves. Lehman Caves is located 5.5 miles up from the nearby town of Baker while Great Basin is north of the city and they're both open every day, all year long, from 8.00 a.m. to 4.00 p.m. For more information, you can call (775) 234-7520 (Operating Hours & Seasons - Great Basin National Park, 2023).

Best Times to Visit

The best times to visit Great Basin National Park are summer and fall. Summer in the park is warm and not too hot, as temperatures vary between 50 °F and 77 °F in June and 55 °F to 85 °F in July and August (Lokvenec, 2023b). June is also the month with the longest days and least rainfall, so it's the perfect time to take a tour. People prefer visiting the park during the summer months because they're more likely to spot the Milky Way during a clear night. However, this means that summer is also the busiest season when accommodation prices go up and there are more visitors.

For these reasons, you might prefer going between September and November, when temperatures are still comfortable enough to enjoy your trip. In September, temperatures range between 47 °F and 74 °F, while in October, they fall between 37 °F and 61 °F, and in November, they get as low as 25 °F. Therefore, you might prefer visiting the park in September or October. We absolutely discourage you from going to Great Basin in winter. Temperatures keep dropping, snow might fall during your visit, the Scenic Road is closed, and days are much shorter (Lokvenec, 2023b).

How to Get There

Car

Great Basin National Park is located about five miles west of the town of Baker and is an extremely remote area, so it's not easy to reach. You'll have limited services, no public Wi-Fi, and no cell coverage. For all of these reasons, you must prepare well and plan accordingly. In addition, GPS navigation doesn't work properly, so it might guide you into even more remote areas. Therefore, you must follow the directions below.

- **From the east or west:** From US Highway 6 & 50, turn south on Nevada State Highway 487 and reach Baker. Then, turn west on Highway 488 and travel five miles.

- **From Nevada:** Travel north on US Highway 93, also called Great Basin Highway. At the junction of US Highway 6 & 50, drive east to

Nevada State Highway 487 and turn south and travel for five miles to reach Baker.

- **From Utah:** Travel north on Utah State Highway 21 until it becomes Nevada State Highway 487 as you cross the border. Turn west on Highway 488 until you reach Baker and then, the park.

Plane

If you want to take the plane, you don't have many alternatives. The nearest airports are Cedar City Regional Airport, which is about 140 miles away from Great Basin, and St. George Regional Airport, which is a bit more than 200 miles away. They both provide limited flights and you can't rent a car or RV there, so plan your trip accordingly.

Another option is to take a flight to Salt Lake City in Utah, which is about 230 miles from the park, or to Las Vegas, which is about 280 miles from Great Basin. Both airports offer all the services you would need, including car rentals. If you want to take a flight and then rent a car, we suggest you fly to Salt Lake City or Las Vegas. If you plan to rent a car or RV without spending too much money, remember you can always check the Turo app to rent from locals.

You must also keep in mind public transportation is not available in the area of Great Basin National Park, so you must travel there with a private vehicle.

Accommodations

As you might have already realized, you won't find many services inside the park. Therefore, you'll need to stay in one of the nearby cities.

- **Stargazer Inn & Bristlecone General Store:** It's located in Baker and provides a hotel, RV sites, and a general store where you can find everything you need. It's open from spring through fall and is also pet-friendly, so your fur friend is welcome! For more information, you can call (775) 234-7323.

- **End of the Trail...er:** It's located at Page and Eureka, in Baker and provides just two bedrooms with a kitchenette, but it's absolutely worth it. You'll have an incredible view over the park and take some time for yourself to relax and stay away from crowds and traffic. It's open from May to October.

- **Whispering Elms Motel, Campground, & RV Park:** It's located in Baker and perfect if you prefer rustic and peaceful accommodations! This place provides camping, tent, and RV sites, so there's a spot for everyone. It's open from spring to the end of October. For more information, you can call (775) 234-9900.

- **The Border Inn:** It's 13 miles from the park and provides everything you need. It's a hotel casino and RV park with 22 campsites, a restaurant, gas, diesel, a convenience store, and much more! It's open all year. For more information, you can call (775) 234-7300.

- **Sacramento Pass (BLM):** It's located 15 miles north of Baker, it's open all year, and provides RV and tent sites. For more information, you can call (775) 289-1800.

- **Hidden Canyon Ranch:** It's located 14 miles south of Baker and provides rooms with all the amenities you need, including an outdoor barbecue, a free book exchange, and a covered patio. It's open all year. For more information, you can call (775) 234-7172.

- **Major's Station RV Park:** It's located 40 miles away from the park, in the direction of the town of Ely. It's open all year and provides RV and tent sites. For more information, you can call (775) 591-0347.

- **Camping inside the park:** If you want to camp inside Great Basin, you can choose among six different campgrounds. You'll find the Lower Lehman Creek Campground, Upper Lehman Creek Campground, Wheeler Peak Campground, Baker Creek Campground, and Grey Cliffs Campground. Potable water is not available in any of the campgrounds, and they're not always open. For specific information on each campground, you can visit www.nps.gov.

Keep in mind you can always check Airbnb and Vrbo for more accommodations in the area.

Restaurants, Goods, and Services

Inside the park, the visitor centers are the only places that provide basic services and shops. You can find a bookstore in each one and the Great Basin Cafe and Gift Shop at the Lehman Cave visitor center. The shop is open from April to October, from 8.00 a.m. to 5.00 p.m. For more information, you can call (775) 234-7200. Outside the park, you have plenty of opportunities to have a delicious meal and refresh after a long hike!

Sugar, Salt and Malt: It's located in Baker and famous for its pastries! You'll eat amazing cakes and cookies and have a tasty coffee. The restaurant is open for lunch and dinner. You'll find it at 70 S Baker Avenue, Baker. For more information, you can call (719) 237-5726.

- **Sugar, Salt and Malt:** It's located in Baker and famous for its pastries! You'll eat amazing cakes and cookies and have a tasty coffee. The restaurant is open for lunch and dinner. You'll find it at 70 S Baker Avenue, Baker. For more information, you can call (719) 237-5726.

- **Sandra's Mexican Food:** It's a food truck open for lunch and dinner that keeps varying working hours. You can find it at 45 Pioche Street, Baker.

- **487 Grill:** It's located at 487 Grill 120 Baker Avenue, in Baker and provides excellent breakfast, lunch, and dinner. It's open from Wednesday to Saturday. For more information, you can call (775) 456-0056.

- **Baker Sinclair Gas Station:** To fill the tank, you can go to Baker Sinclair Gas Station, which also provides restrooms, a laundromat, and showers. The gas station is open 24/7. For more information, you can call (775) 234-7316.

Breweries and Wineries

Unfortunately, you won't find many breweries or wineries close to Great Basin, so you'll have to drive for a while to get a taste of Nevada's craft beer and wine. You find a list of the most recommended breweries and wineries below!

- **Tonopah Brewing Company:** Located at 315 South Main Street,

Tonopah.

- **Midtown Wine Bar:** Located at 1527 South Virginia St., Reno.

- **Sanders Family Winery:** Located at 3780 E Kellogg Road, Pahrump.

- **Basin & Range Cellars:** Located at 415 E. 4th Street (Unit B), Reno.

- **Shoe Tree Brewing Company:** Located at 1496 Old Hot Springs Road, Carson City.

- **Kruze RD Winery:** Located at 250 Kruze Road, Lovelock.

- **Black Rabbit Mead Co.:** Located at 401 East 4th Street, Reno.

Rules and Regulations

If you want to bring your pet with you, be aware pets aren't allowed in many areas of Great Basin, so your visit will be highly affected and you'll have to limit your activities. Pets are allowed inside the park only if they have a leash that is not longer than six feet. Pets aren't permitted at evening programs, in Lehman Caves, and on many hiking trails. The only two exceptions are Lexington Arch Trail and the hike that goes from Baker to Great Basin visitor center. In addition, pets can never be left unattended, not even in campgrounds.

History and Trivia

The first inhabitants of the area of Great Basin were the Fremont people, who lived across Utah, Colorado, and Nevada between 1000 and 1300 (Pattiz, 2023d). Their name derives from the Fremont River of Utah where remains of their culture were first found, but they also left many signs of occupation in Great Basin.

An interesting fact about the park that you'll find surprising if you like nature and plants is that you can find some of the oldest trees in the world here (Pattiz, 2023d). In particular, the rare Great Basin bristlecone pine can live for more than 4,000 years even in extremely harsh conditions! Inside the park, you can also find the remains of the oldest tree on Earth, which was called the Prometheus Tree and lived for about 5,000 years (Pattiz, 2023d).

In addition to the some of the oldest trees, the park also includes the second highest peak in Nevada, which is Wheeler Peak, more than 13,000 feet high. Another interesting fact about Great Basin is that it is the best place to gaze at the stars at night! That's because light pollution and humidity is minimal, so the sky is very dark. If you camp inside the park, take the opportunity to get out of your tent or vehicle and look at the stars above you for a while (Pattiz, 2023d).

Scenic Drives and Overlooks

The only scenic drive at Great Basin National Park is Wheeler Peak, which is absolutely amazing! It's a true mountain road that will leave you in awe of the stunning views over the park and even the Great Basin Desert. Wheeler Peak drive is only 12 miles long and will make you gain over 4,000 feet in elevation. It's like driving into the clouds and you'll be surprised by all the scenic changes in just 12 miles. You'll probably meet mule deer, coyotes, and marmots along the way.

- **Look at the sagebrush oceans:** If you start the scenic drive at Lehman Cave Visitor Center, you'll drive through a typical eco-region of the area made of sagebrush. If you're lucky enough to drive through it during a summer rain, you can smell the sage. So nice!

- **Pass through the pinyon woodland:** You'll be at an elevation of 8,000 feet and notice how the landscape changes. After sagebrush, you'll see pinyon pines that have edible nuts.

- **Be amazed by the curl-leaf mountain mahogany:** It's a species of tree that looks rough and scrappy.

- **View the collection of conifers:** This is the next eco-region you'll see along the road.

- **Glance at the aspens:** At the end of the road, you'll reach an elevation of 10,000 feet where you'll be surrounded by aspens, part of a subalpine forest that is typical of the Rocky Mountains.

Along the road, you'll find many parking areas where you can stop and just enjoy the views.

Things to Do in the Park

You can choose among plenty of activities to do inside the park. You'll find a list below.

- **Lehman Caves Tours:** You must absolutely do a tour of the Lehman Caves! Lehman Caves is the longest cave system in the whole state and a magical experience. You can't visit the caves by yourself, so you have to buy a ticket and participate in a ranger-guided tour. During summer, you can try both the Lodge Room and Grand Palace tours while in winter you can only do the Lodge Room. Check the website www.nps.gov for more information on safety, schedules, reservations, and everything you need to know.

- **Explore nature around you:** Some popular activities in the park include bird watching, stargazing, and wildflower viewing. The best places to spot birds are the campgrounds inside the park and the Wheeler Peak Scenic Drive. As we already mentioned, Great Basin is perfect for stargazing! You can watch the stars on your own or participate in astronomy programs. The perfect places to discover amazing flowers are the Wheeler Peak Scenic Drive, Island Forest, and Baker Creek trails.

- **RV/auto touring:** In addition to Wheeler Peak, you can drive through Baker Creek, Strawberry, Snake, and Lexington Arch roads. Check road conditions and closures before going. Among them,

Lexington Arch Road is the roughest one, so make sure to have the appropriate vehicle.

- **Winter touring:** Even if winter isn't the best time to visit the park, you can still try some activities, like snowshoeing and skiing.

- **Wild caves:** Inside the park, you can find more than 40 caves! Several of them are open for recreational purposes but you must get a permit first.

- **Horseback riding and pack animals:** You can visit the park by horse, llama, mule, or burro! However, you can't ride on the paved road and a few trails. For more information, you can check www.nps. gov.

- **Fishing:** If you want to fish, the most popular locations are Lehman Creek, Snake Creek, and Baker Creek.

Hiking Trails

Inside Great Basin, there are many hiking trails! You'll find a list with some of the most popular hikes below.

- **Sky Islands Forest Trail:** It's an easy 4.0-mile trail accessible by anyone. It begins at Bristlecone parking lot and leads to a stunning alpine conifer forest.

- **Mountain View Nature Trail:** It's an easy 0.3-mile loop trail that can be considered a leisurely walk through nature.

- **Alpine Lakes Loop:** It's an easy 2.7-mile hike that is accessible by anyone and provides spectacular views of Wheeler Peak. It also passes the alpine lakes called Stella and Teresa.

- **Bristlecone Grove:** It's a moderate 2.8-mile trail that allows you to walk through an ancient forest.

- **Serviceberry Loop:** It's a moderate 3.2-mile loop trail that provides stunning views over the park at over 9,000 feet of elevation.

- **Pole Canyon Trail:** It's a moderate 3.9-mile trail that crosses Baker Creek and Pole Canyon. It's a gem of a hike!

Surrounding Treasures

Let's look at some of the surrounding treasures you can't miss if you decide to visit Great Basin National Park!

- **Loneliest Road in America:** It's just 11 minutes away from Great Basin and is also known as Highway 50. Along the way, you'll find small towns to stop by and get a taste of what the area has to offer.

- **Ward Charcoal Ovens State Historic Park:** It's just a bit more than one hour away. This can be a quick stop if you're just curious to see it or a must-see if you enjoy gazing at the stars.

- **Cave Lake State Park:** It's 64 miles from the park, and provides plenty of water activities if that is something you enjoy!

- **Ely:** It's the closest big town, a bit more than one hour away from the park. For more information about the town, you can visit www. elynevada.net.

- **Cathedral Gorge State Park:** It's a bit less than two hours from Great

Basin and provides stunning views of rock formations. You can also walk through formations that resemble slot canyons.

In this chapter, you learned some of the most interesting facts about Great Basin National Park. If you want to visit the park, you must go in summer or fall, although we suggest you go in fall as summer might get busy and crowded. You also discovered that the area doesn't provide many services, so you must plan your trip accordingly and rent a vehicle to get to the park and sleep and eat outside of it. You also learned about the most beautiful scenic drive in the park, which is the Wheeler Peak, and the Lehman Caves Tours, which you can't miss! Finally, we looked at some of the most popular hiking trails and hidden gems around the park. At this point, our journey has come to an end! We have visited some of the lesser known national parks of the USA and now you just have to decide which one (or ones!) you'll visit first. Are you craving additional information on even lonelier national parks? You'll find **two bonus parks** in the conclusion.

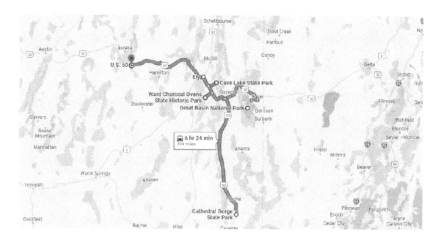

CONCLUSION

Tell me, what is it you plan to do with your one wild precious life? -Mary Oliver

In this book, we focused on some of the lesser-known and loneliest national parks in the USA. We started our journey at Badlands National Park, then visited Shenandoah, Capitol Reef, Voyageurs, North Cascades, Guadalupe, and Great Basin. For each national park, we discussed fun and historical facts to help you understand a bit more about the area and the people who inhabited it for millennia. We also discussed the basic information you'll need to locate the parks and move around without issues. For example, we mentioned the visitor centers of each park and how to reach them by plane and car. In most cases, you'll have to rent a car or drive your own vehicle, so plan accordingly.

Next, we listed all accommodations, restaurants, and various goods and services inside and outside the national parks. In some cases, like Shenandoah and Voyageurs, you have plenty of opportunities to sleep and eat inside the park. In other cases, such as Guadalupe and Great Basin, you'll have to find a place in one of the cities nearby. However, you'll always have the chance to stay in campgrounds inside the parks and enjoy a night out in the wild, looking at the stars!

After some basic and practical information, we dove deep into the activities you can do inside each park, including hiking trails. You sometimes have the chance to visit the park by horse or other pack animals and try activities that are specific to each park. You also learned about rules and regulations, especially concerning pets. You must keep in mind pets aren't often welcome inside national parks for their own protection. Wild animals roam free and might attack your fur friend or cause trouble. In any case, you'll always find some trails and areas where you can walk your pet on a leash.

Finally, we didn't stop at telling you everything about each national park, but also provided some advice on what to explore nearby. We highlighted some areas of interest, like cities to roam around and other parks or attractions worth visiting. You now have all the information you need to travel by yourself, with your partner, or even a friend or two—adventure awaits!

If you feel like the national parks discussed in this book aren't enough, you can also visit **Dry Tortugas National Park in Florida and Congaree National Park in South Carolina.**

The address for Dry Tortugas is 40001 SR-9336, Homestead, Florida 33034. It's a remote, 100-square mile national park where you can find a 19th century fort named Fort Jefferson (Dry Tortugas National Park, 2016). An interesting fact about this park is that you can only visit it by boat or seaplane, as it's mainly composed of open water and tiny islands. There, you can spot some beautiful birds and magnificent coral reefs as well as marine life. If you love crystal clear, blue water and enjoy snorkeling, this is the place.

Alternatively, you can visit **Congaree National Park.** The address is 100 National Park Road, Hopkins 29061, South Carolina. It's an amazing place that offers breathtaking views, astonishing biodiversity, and a rich ecosystem. It's absolutely incredible! There, you'll find wonderful trails in the middle of forests surrounded by water. We, Beatrix and Zia, wanted to include Congaree National Park because it's a surprisingly perfect place to enjoy fall foliage (we're huge fall foliage fans)! This park lies in the heart of South Carolina and is relatively unknown when it comes to fall foliage. The cypress trees shed their rusty leaves into the swamps and the bright red tupelo trees show off their red and gold leaves against the bright blue skies. This park promises some quiet autumn bliss away from the crowds if fall colors are your thing but chaos is not.

Now, it is time to plan your next adventure! Where will you go first? The USA is chock-full of wondrous destinations and many are still very much a secret. There is still no shortage of special places to enjoy without the crowds and the chaos more common in more well-known parks. Please share your tips, feedback, and photos as you explore our featured places and spaces.

We would appreciate your ideas for future travel guides. We have a few, but always welcome your thoughts. Messages can be left at @worldofwander on Instagram or Beatrix Zia on Facebook. You can even email us at worldofwonderexplore@gmail.com—we welcome your feedback and look forward to hearing from you.

We have loved this opportunity to share some of our favorite lesser-known national parks and surrounding areas with you. They contain all of the magic but none of the madness associated with the more traveled parks! Thank you for appreciating and using this lovingly and carefully curated national park travel guide.

Where will you wander next my friend?

Safe Travels,
Beatrix & Zia
Now that you have everything you need to take these incredible national parks and some of the surrounding areas by storm, it's time to pass on

your new found knowledge and show other readers where they can find the same help.

Simply by leaving your honest opinion of this book on Amazon, you'll show other national park and nature enthusiasts where they can find the information they're looking for, and pass their passion for adventure forward.

Thank you for your help. Joy filled and worry free travel is kept alive when we pass on our knowledge – and you're helping us to do just that.

AUTHOR BIO

Beatrix & Zia are lifelong friends and travel companions who met in high school in Richmond, Virginia. Upon meeting, they quickly bonded over their intense curiosity about the world and their deep desire to learn through travel!

Since then, they have had many adventures, both together and apart. Between them, they have five children ranging in age from 18 to 30. While raising their children they continued to travel (with their kiddos alongside) as they both agree that the best education comes from experiencing the world firsthand.

Now once again on their own, they are off exploring with renewed vigor. Through traveling, Beatrix has developed the hobbies that will carry her through life, including photography, hiking, cycling, and kayaking. Zia's favorite pastimes are cooking, trying new cuisines, walking in picturesque places, and designing world-inspired children's fashion. You can view her works at www.zianyc.com.

Zia is currently an entrepreneur, as well as a banker working in Manhattan, New York, and Beatrix resides near Denver, Colorado, and works in non-profit leadership. For both of them, this is their first book.

REFERENCES

"If you truly love nature, you will find beauty everywhere." - Laura Ingalls Wilder. (n.d.). Pinterest. https://www.pinterest.com/pin/128807180179684557/

1 way to travel from Provo Airport (PVU) to Capitol Reef National Park. (n.d.). Rome2Rio. https://www.rome2rio.com/map/Provo-Airport-PVU/Capitol-Reef-National-Park

1 way to travel from St. George Regional Airport (SGU) to Capitol Reef National Park. (n.d.). Rome2Rio. https://www.rome2rio.com/map/St-George-Regional-Airport-SGU/Capitol-Reef-National-Park

2 ways to travel from Grand Junction Airport (GJT) to Capitol Reef National Park. (n.d.). Rome2Rio. https://www.rome2rio.com/map/Grand-Junction-Airport-GJT/Capitol-Reef-National-Park

25 best grocery stores near Capitol Reef National Park in Torrey. (n.d.). Kupino.com. https://www.kupino.com/shopping-near/capitol-reef-national-park

34 best stops between North Cascades National Park and Olympic National Park. (n.d.). Wanderlog. https://wanderlog.com/drive/between/59700/59025/north-cascades-national-park-to-olympic-national-park-drive

4 ways to travel from Salt Lake City Airport (SLC) to Capitol Reef National Park. (n.d.). Rome2Rio. https://www.rome2rio.com/map/Salt-Lake-City-Airport-SLC/Capitol-Reef-National-Park

A better Badlands base camp. (n.d.). Badlands Hotel & Campground.

https://badlandshotelandcampground.com/?utm_
source=badlandsinteriorcampground.com&utm_
medium=referral&utm_campaign=bhc-campground-legacy-
doman-redirect

A place to come relax, hunt and escape. (n.d.). Whispering Pines Outfitters. https://whisperingpinesoutfitters.com/

A quote by E.B. White. (n.d.). Good Reads. https://www.goodreads.com/quotes/33989-always-be-on-the-lookout-for-the-presence-of-wonder

Adventure In Winthrop. (n.d.). Winthrop Washington. https://winthropwashington.com/

Amy. (2021, August 23). *Pet friendly breweries and wineries in South Dakota's Black Hills.* GoPetFriendly. https://www.gopetfriendly.com/blog/pet-friendly-breweries-and-wineries-in-south-dakotas-black-hills/

Anna. (2021, November 10). *7 breweries near Shenandoah National Park.* Stuck on the Go. https://www.stuckonthego.com/breweries-near-shenandoah-national-park/

Appalachian Trail Conservancy. (2022, March 8). *"The forest is a quiet place and nature is beautiful. I don't want to sit and rock. I want to do something." - Emma "Grandma" Gatewood.* X. https://twitter.com/at_conservancy/status/1501256444615618564

Auto touring - Great Basin National Park. (2023, August 24). National Park Service. https://www.nps.gov/grba/planyourvisit/auto-touring.htm

Badland's Travel Stop. (n.d.). Yelp. https://www.yelp.com/biz/badlands-travel-stop-kadoka

Badlands National Park rules & regulations. (n.d.). AllTrips. https://www.

allblackhills.com/badlands_national_park/rules_regulations.php

Badlands sunrises & sunsets. (2020, December 29). National Park Service. https://www.nps.gov/thingstodo/badl-sunrises-sunsets.htm

Barren Ridge Vineyards. (n.d.). Barren Ridge. https://www.barrenridgevineyards.com/

Basic information - Badlands National Park. (2021, April 23). National Park Service. https://www.nps.gov/badl/planyourvisit/basicinfo.htm

Basic information - Capitol Reef National Park. (2022, January 2). National Park Service. https://www.nps.gov/care/planyourvisit/basicinfo.htm

Basic information - Guadalupe Mountains National Park. (2023, March 17). National Park Service. https://www.nps.gov/gumo/planyourvisit/basicinfo.htm

Basic information - North Cascades National Park. (2022, August 22). National Park Service. https://www.nps.gov/noca/planyourvisit/basicinfo.htm

Basic information - Voyageurs National Park. (2021, March 3). National Park Service. https://www.nps.gov/voya/planyourvisit/basicinfo.htm

Best gas stations near Capitol Reef National Park in Fruita, UT. (n.d.). Yelp. https://www.yelp.com/search?cflt=servicestations&find_near=capitol-reef-national-park-torrey

Best grocery near Capitol Reef National Park in Fruita, UT. (n.d.). Yelp. https://www.yelp.com/search?cflt=grocery&find_near=capitol-reef-national-park-fruita-2

Best things to do in North Cascades National Park in October (Updated 2023). (n.d.). Trip.com. https://www.trip.com/travel-guide/attraction/north-cascades-national-park-41589/tourist-attractions/type-wineries-distilleries-71-38554/

Best times to visit Shenandoah National Park. (n.d.). U.S. News. https://travel.usnews.com/Shenandoah_National_Park_VA/When_To_Visit/

Best trails in Guadalupe Mountains National Park. (n.d.). AllTrails. https://www.alltrails.com/parks/us/texas/guadalupe-mountains-national-park

Best trails in Shenandoah National Park. (n.d.). AllTrails. https://www.alltrails.com/parks/us/virginia/shenandoah-national-park

Best Western Plains Motel. (n.d.). Best Western Hotels & Resorts. https://www.bestwestern.com/en_US/book/hotels-in-wall/best-western-plains-motel/propertyCode.42022.html

Black Hills & Mount Rushmore vacation deals. (n.d.). Black Hills Vacations. https://www.blackhillsvacations.com/

Black Hills car rentals. (n.d.). Travel South Dakota. https://www.travelsouthdakota.com/sioux-falls/transportation/car-rental/black-hills-car-rentals

Black Hills of Wyoming Region. (n.d.). Black Hills & Badlands. https://www.blackhillsbadlands.com/region/wyoming

Black Hills visitor information center. (n.d.). Black Hills and Badlands SD. https://www.blackhillsbadlands.com/business/black-hills-visitor-information-center

Boating - North Cascades National Park. (2023, May 31). National Park Service. https://www.nps.gov/noca/planyourvisit/boating-and-fishing.htm

Book your vacation rentals: cottages, studios, villas & more. (2019). Vrbo. https://www.vrbo.com/

Bram. (2020, April 20). *Top things to see & do in Shenandoah National Park,*

Virginia. The National Parks Experience. https://www.travel-experience-live.com/5-reasons-visit-shenandoah-national-park-virginia/

Bram. (2021, September 26). *20 best overlooks and views in Shenandoah National Park.* The National Parks Experience. https://www.travel-experience-live.com/best-overlooks-views-in-shenandoah-national-park/

Bram. (2022, March 12). *A guide to accommodation in Shenandoah National Park.* The National Parks Experience. https://www.travel-experience-live.com/shenandoah-national-park-accommodation-lodging-cabins/

Bram. (2023, February 24). *ALL 16 scenic overlooks in Badlands National Park (with photos!).* The National Parks Experience. https://www.travel-experience-live.com/all-scenic-overlooks-in-badlands-national-park-photos/

Campgrounds - Badlands National Park. (2021, July 1). National Park Service. https://www.nps.gov/thingstodo/campgrounds-badl.htm

Campgrounds - Great Basin National Park. (2023, June 16). National Park Service. https://www.nps.gov/grba/planyourvisit/campgrounds.htm

Camping - Guadalupe Mountains National Park. (2022, March 27). National Park Service. https://www.nps.gov/gumo/planyourvisit/camping.htm

Camping - North Cascades National Park. (2023, September 28). National Park Service. https://www.nps.gov/noca/planyourvisit/camping.htm

Camping at Voyageurs National Park. (2023, March 14). National Park

Service. https://www.nps.gov/voya/planyourvisit/camping.htm

Camping in Capitol Reef - Capitol Reef National Park. (2021, August 15). National Park Service. https://www.nps.gov/care/planyourvisit/campinga.htm

Camping options outside the park - Guadalupe Mountains National Park. (2023, January 26). National Park Service. https://www.nps.gov/gumo/planyourvisit/camping-options-outside-the-park.htm

Canyonlands National Park. (2016). National Park Service. https://www.nps.gov/cany/index.htm

Capitol Reef history. (n.d.). Capitol Reef Country. https://capitolreefcountry.com/capitol-reef-national-park-history/

Capitol Reef hotels & lodging. (2023). Utah.com. https://www.utah.com/destinations/national-parks/capitol-reef-national-park/places-to-stay/

Casey's Auto Rental. (n.d.). Travel South Dakota. https://www.travelsouthdakota.com/rapid-city/transportation/car-rental/caseys-auto-rental

Central Hills Region. (n.d.). Black Hills & Badlands. https://www.blackhillsbadlands.com/region/central-hills

Cities near Voyageurs National Park. (n.d.). Tourist Link. https://www.touristlink.com/united-states/voyageurs-national-park/cat/cities.html

Claude Monet Quotes. (n.d.). Brainy Quote. https://www.brainyquote.com/quotes/claude_monet_802612

Coffee Landing Cafe. (n.d.). TripAdvisor. https://www.tripadvisor.com/Restaurant_Review-g60986-d3322987-Reviews-Coffee_

Landing_Cafe-International_Falls_Minnesota.html

Congaree National Park. (2023, February 23). National Park Service. https://www.nps.gov/cong/index.htm

Cowboy Corner. (n.d.). Travel South Dakota. https://www.travelsouthdakota.com/interior/food-drink/cafediner/cowboy-corner

Coyles Standard Service. (n.d.). Yelp. https://www.yelp.com/biz/coyles-standard-service-philip

Derr, A. (2014, August 15). *Plan a visit to the Guadalupe Mountains National Park in Texas.* Scouting Magazine. https://scoutingmagazine.org/2014/08/plan-visit-guadalupe-mountains-national-park/#:~:text=This%20darkened%20corner%20of%20West

Dierickx, K. (2015). *59 fun facts about our national parks.* Outdoor Project. https://www.outdoorproject.com/articles/59-fun-facts-about-our-national-parks

Dining - Shenandoah National Park. (2021, June 29). National Park Service. https://www.nps.gov/shen/planyourvisit/dining.htm

Dining. (n.d.). Capitol Reef Country. https://capitolreefcountry.com/dining/

Directions - Capitol Reef National Park. (2022, January 3). National Park Service. https://www.nps.gov/care/planyourvisit/directions.htm

Directions - Great Basin National Park. (2023, August 22). National Park Service. https://home.nps.gov/grba/planyourvisit/directions.htm

Directions - Guadalupe Mountains National Park. (2023, March 23). National Park Service. https://www.nps.gov/gumo/

planyourvisit/directions.htm

Directions - North Cascades National Park. (2022, June 14). National Park Service. https://www.nps.gov/noca/planyourvisit/directions. htm

Directions - Shenandoah National Park. (2022, November 12). National Park Service. https://www.nps.gov/shen/planyourvisit/ directions.htm

Discover Concrete, Washington. (n.d.). Concrete Chamber of Commerce. https://concrete-wa.com/

Drive around the South Unit of the Badlands. (2020, December 30). National Park Service. https://www.nps.gov/thingstodo/badl-south-unit-drive.htm

Drive Sage Creek Rim Road. (2020, December 30). National Park Service. https://www.nps.gov/thingstodo/sage-creek-rim-road.htm

Dry Tortugas National Park. (2016). National Park Service. https://www. nps.gov/drto/index.htm

Eating & sleeping - Voyageurs National Park. (2022, December 21). National Park Service. https://www.nps.gov/voya/ planyourvisit/eatingsleeping.htm

Econo Lodge. (n.d.). Choice Hotels. https://www. choicehotels.com/south-dakota/wall/econo-lodge-hotels/sd050?adults=2&checkInDate=2023-11-09&checkOutDate=2023-11-11

Emma Gatewood. (n.d.). Appalachian Trail History. https:// appalachiantrailhistory.org/exhibits/show/hikers/gatewood

Enjoy the night sky. (2021, July 2). National Park Service. https://www. nps.gov/thingstodo/night-sky-badl.htm

Entrance passes. (2019). National Park Service. https://www.nps.gov/

planyourvisit/passes.htm

Esther & Jacob. (2017, July 26). *7 things you can't miss in Great Basin National Park Nevada*. Local Adventurer. https://localadventurer.com/great-basin-national-park-nevada/

Exxon. (n.d.). Yelp. https://www.yelp.com/biz/exxon-wall-2

Facts, history, and wildlife of Badlands National Park. (2019, July 8). Reboot. https://www.foreverresorts.com/blog/2019/07/facts-history-and-wildlife-of-badlands-national-park

Fees & passes - Capitol Reef National Park. (2023, August 17). National Park Service. https://www.nps.gov/care/planyourvisit/fees.htm

Fees & passes - Great Basin National Park. (2023, August 19). National Park Service. https://www.nps.gov/grba/planyourvisit/fees.htm

Fees & passes - Shenandoah National Park. (2023, May 30). National Park Service. https://www.nps.gov/shen/planyourvisit/fees.htm

Find your drive. (n.d.). Turo. https://turo.com/

Fishing - Great Basin National Park. (2021, October 30). National Park Service. https://www.nps.gov/grba/planyourvisit/fishing.htm

Getting to Badlands National Park. (2022, September 23). Nationalparked. com. https://www.nationalparked.com/badlands/directions-flights-maps

Goblin Valley State Park. (n.d.). Utah Life Elevated. https://www.visitutah.com/Places-To-Go/Parks-Outdoors/Goblin-Valley

Goods & services - Great Basin National Park. (2023, September 15). National Park Service. https://www.nps.gov/grba/planyourvisit/goodsandservices.htm

Goods & services - Shenandoah National Park. (2023, May 31). National Park Service. https://www.nps.gov/shen/planyourvisit/goods-services.htm

Helling, A. (2023, July 20). *The best time to visit Badlands National Park in 2023.* Travellers Worldwide. https://travellersworldwide.com/best-time-to-visit-badlands-national-park/

Hiking Badlands back roads with your dog. (2021, April 19). National Park Service. https://www.nps.gov/thingstodo/badl-dogs-on-back-roads.htm

Hiking the Badlands. (2020, December 30). National Park Service. https://www.nps.gov/thingstodo/hiking-badl.htm

Hiking trails - Great Basin National Park. (2023, July 23). National Park Service. https://www.nps.gov/grba/planyourvisit/hiking-information.htm

Hiking trails - Voyageurs National Park. (2022, July 18). National Park Service. https://www.nps.gov/voya/planyourvisit/hiking-trails.htm

Horseback riding & pack animals - Great Basin National Park. (2023, August 13). National Park Service. https://www.nps.gov/grba/planyourvisit/pack-animals.htm

Horseback riding in the Badlands. (2022, December 1). National Park Service. https://www.nps.gov/thingstodo/horseback-riding-badl.htm

Hussain, A. (2023, May 31). *The ultimate guide to Guadalupe Mountains National Park - best things to do, see & enjoy!* Upgraded Points. https://upgradedpoints.com/travel/guadalupe-mountains-national-park-travel-guide/

I-90 East Region. (n.d.). Black Hills & Badlands. https://www.blackhillsbadlands.com/region/i-90-east

Isle Royale National Park. (2016). National Park Service. https://www.nps.gov/isro/index.htm

Jack's Campers. (n.d.). Jack's Campers. https://www.jackscampers.com/

John Muir quotes. (n.d.). Brainy Quote. https://www.brainyquote.com/quotes/john_muir_108391

Julie. (2019, January 13). *Best things to do in Dead Horse Point State Park.* Earth Trekkers. https://www.earthtrekkers.com/best-things-to-do-dead-horse-point-state-park-utah/

Julie. (2020, September 22). *9 best things to do in North Cascades National Park.* Earth Trekkers. https://www.earthtrekkers.com/best-things-to-do-in-north-cascades-national-park/

Kadoka Gas & Go. (n.d.). Yelp. https://www.yelp.com/biz/kadoka-gas-and-go-kadoka-2

Kennedy, B. N. (2021, February 23). *The 9 best towns in the Shenandoah Valley.* TripSavvy. https://www.tripsavvy.com/the-best-towns-in-the-shenandoah-valley-5112948

Kroeger, K. (2021, November 11). *15 best things to do in Voyageurs National Park.* Via Travelers. https://viatravelers.com/things-to-do-in-voyageurs-national-park/

Lake Park Campground and Cottages. (n.d.). Lake Park Campground & Cottages. https://lakeparkcampground.com/

Lakota. (n.d.). Black Hills & Badlands. https://www.blackhillsbadlands.com/lakota

Lawrence, K. (2023, April 4). *The scenic drive to Guadalupe Mountains National Park in Texas is almost as beautiful as the destination itself.* Only in Your State. https://www.onlyinyourstate.com/texas/scenic-drive-beautiful-destination-tx/

Lehman Caves Tours - Great Basin National Park. (2023, October 27). National Park Service. https://www.nps.gov/grba/planyourvisit/lehman-caves-tours.htm

Lokvenec, S. (2023a, April 11). *Best time to visit Voyageurs National Park in 2023*. Travellers Worldwide. https://travellersworldwide.com/best-time-to-visit-voyageurs-national-park/

Lokvenec, S. (2023b, May 22). *The best time to Visit Great Basin National Park in 2023*. Travellers Worldwide. https://travellersworldwide.com/best-time-to-visit-great-basin-national-park/

Longe, P. (2022, August 12). *Best time to visit Badlands National Park (dramatic landscapes!)*. Town & Tourist. https://www.townandtourist.com/best-time-to-visit-badlands-national-park/

Marblemount Diner. (n.d.). TripAdvisor. https://www.tripadvisor.com/Restaurant_Review-g58590-d599331-Reviews-Marblemount_Diner-Marblemount_Washington.html

Marblemount. (n.d.). Scenic Washington. https://scenicwa.com/poi/marblemount

Mazama. (n.d.). Scenic Washington. https://www.scenicwa.com/poi/mazama

Mecelin. (2022, April 11). *Top 10 unbelievable facts about the Badlands National Park*. Discover Walks Blog. https://www.discoverwalks.com/blog/united-states/top-10-unbelievable-facts-about-the-badlands-national-park/

Melroy, J. (2022, June 18). *Where to stay in Shenandoah National Park? 17 best Shenandoah hotels in 2022*. National Park Obsessed. https://nationalparkobsessed.com/where-to-stay-in-shenandoah-hotels/#6-best-places-to-stay-in-shenandoah-national-park

Mondo Restaurant. (n.d.). TripAdvisor. https://www.tripadvisor.com/Restaurant_Review-g58590-d3393008-Reviews-Mondo_Restaurant-Marblemount_Washington.html

Montana Cafe. (n.d.). Yelp. https://www.yelp.com/biz/montana-cafe-cook

Nearby attractions. (n.d.). Mount Rushmore National Memorial. https://www.mtrushmorenationalmemorial.com/things-to-do/nearby-attractions/

Nicole. (2023, June 7). *The 9 best cities and towns near Capitol Reef National Park.* Nichole the Nomad. https://nicholethenomad.com/travel-blog/towns-near-capitol-reef-national-park

North Cascades Lodge at Stehekin. (n.d.). North Cascades Lodge at Stehekin. https://lodgeatstehekin.com/

Northern High Plains Region. (n.d.). Black Hills & Badlands. https://www.blackhillsbadlands.com/region/northern-high-plains

Northern Hills Region. (n.d.). Black Hills & Badlands. https://www.blackhillsbadlands.com/region/northern-hills

Nudd, A. (2023, May 26). *How to get to Badlands National Park (best airports and roads).* Dirt in My Shoes. https://www.dirtinmyshoes.com/how-to-get-to-badlands-national-park-best-airports-and-roads/

Oliver, M. (n.d.). *The summer day.* Library of Congress. https://www.loc.gov/programs/poetry-and-literature/poet-laureate/poet-laureate-projects/poetry-180/all-poems/item/poetry-180-133/the-summer-day/

Olson, K. (2023, March 27). *Minneapolis to Voyageurs National Park: directions, stops, & more (2023).* Kassidy's Journey. https://kassidysjourney.com/minneapolis-to-voyageurs-national-park/

Olympic National Park. (2023, September 11). National Park Service. https://www.nps.gov/olym/index.htm

Operating dates & hours - Shenandoah National Park. (2023, August

7). National Park Service. https://www.nps.gov/shen/
planyourvisit/hours.htm

Operating hours & seasons - Badlands National Park. (2020, October
15). National Park Service. https://www.nps.gov/badl/
planyourvisit/hours.htm

Operating hours & seasons - Capitol Reef National Park. (2023, March
13). National Park Service. https://www.nps.gov/care/
planyourvisit/hours.htm

Operating hours & seasons - Great Basin National Park. (2023, October
7). National Park Service. https://www.nps.gov/grba/
planyourvisit/hours.htm

Our community. (n.d.). Kabetogama Township. https://www.
kabtownship.com/

Park regulations - Voyageurs National Park. (2022, November 9). National
Park Service. https://www.nps.gov/voya/planyourvisit/park-
regulations.htm

Park stores - Voyageurs National Park. (2022, December 19). National Park
Service. https://www.nps.gov/voya/park-stores.htm

Pattiz, J. (2023a, October 4). *Voyageurs National Park: epic guide
to Minnesota's watery wonderland.* More than Just Parks.
https://morethanjustparks.com/voyageurs-national-
park/#:~:text=and%20potential%20challenges.-

Pattiz, T. (2023b, February 3). *10 fascinating facts about Guadalupe
Mountains National Park.* More than Just Parks. https://
morethanjustparks.com/guadalupe-mountains-national-park-
facts/

Pattiz, T. (2023c, March 2). *10 amazing facts about Badlands National
Park.* More than Just Parks. https://morethanjustparks.com/

badlands-national-park-facts/

Pattiz, T. (2023d, May 1). *10 fascinating facts about Great Basin National Park*. More than Just Parks. https://morethanjustparks.com/ great-basin-national-park-facts/

Pattiz, T. (2023e, May 1). *12 surprising facts about Shenandoah National Park*. More than Just Parks. https://morethanjustparks.com/12-surprising-facts-about-shenandoah-national-park/

Pattiz, T. (2023f, May 1). *12 surprising Voyageurs National Park facts*. More than Just Parks. https://morethanjustparks.com/voyageurs-national-park-facts/

Pattiz, T. (2023g, October 4). *12 amazing facts about Capitol Reef National Park*. More than Just Parks. https://morethanjustparks.com/ capitol-reef-facts/

Pattiz, T. (2023h, October 4). *11 fascinating facts about North Cascades National Park to know*. More than Just Parks. https:// morethanjustparks.com/north-cascades-national-park-facts/

Pattiz, W. (2023i, October 4). *15 epic hikes in North Cascades National Park (+1 to skip!)*. More than Just Parks. https://morethanjustparks. com/best-hikes-north-cascades-national-park-trails/

Permits - Great Basin National Park. (2023, August 22). National Park Service. https://www.nps.gov/grba/planyourvisit/permits.htm

Permits & reservations - Capitol Reef National Park. (2023, April 6). National Park Service. https://www.nps.gov/care/ planyourvisit/permitsandreservations.htm

Pets - Capitol Reef National Park. (2022, September 12). National Park Service. https://www.nps.gov/care/planyourvisit/pets.htm

Pets - Great Basin National Park. (2023, September 15). National Park Service. https://www.nps.gov/grba/planyourvisit/pets.htm

Pets - Guadalupe Mountains National Park. (2022, September 19). National Park Service. https://www.nps.gov/gumo/planyourvisit/pets.htm

Pets - North Cascades National Park. (2023, March 28). National Park Service. https://www.nps.gov/noca/planyourvisit/pets.htm

Pets - Shenandoah National Park. (2022, September 14). National Park Service. https://www.nps.gov/shen/planyourvisit/pets.htm

Phillips 66. (n.d.). Yelp. https://www.yelp.com/biz/phillips-66-wall

Public transportation - North Cascades National Park. (2017, July 24). National Park Service. https://www.nps.gov/noca/planyourvisit/publictransportation.htm

Ralph Waldo Emerson quotes. (n.d.-a). Brainy Quote. https://www.brainyquote.com/quotes/ralph_waldo_emerson_106883

Ralph Waldo Emerson quotes. (n.d.-b). Brainy Quote. https://www.brainyquote.com/quotes/ralph_waldo_emerson_125813

Rapid City / Black Hills Koa Holiday. (n.d.). Koa. https://koa.com/campgrounds/rapid-city/

Rapid City. (n.d.). Black Hills & Badlands. https://www.blackhillsbadlands.com/cities-towns/rapid-city

Regulations - Capitol Reef National Park. (2023, August 25). National Park Service. https://www.nps.gov/care/regulations.htm

Restaurants - Great Basin National Park. (2023, June 29). National Park Service. https://www.nps.gov/grba/planyourvisit/restaurants.htm

Restaurants near Voyageurs National Park. (n.d.). Open Table. https://www.opentable.com/landmark/restaurants-near-voyageurs-national-park

Ross Lake Resort. (n.d.). Ross Lake Resort. https://www.rosslakeresort.

com/

RV rental Capitol Reef National Park, UT. (n.d.). Outdoorsy. https://www.outdoorsy.com/rv-rental/utah/capitol-reef-national-park

RV rentals. (2023). Cruise America. https://www.cruiseamerica.com/rv-rentals

Scenic drives - Guadalupe Mountains National Park. (2023, January 10). National Park Service. https://www.nps.gov/gumo/planyourvisit/scenicdrives.htm

Scenic drives. (n.d.). Capitol Reef Country. https://capitolreefcountry.com/scenic-drives/

Seely, H. (2021, September 24). *Top 5 benefits of national parks.* Tamborasi. https://www.tamborasi.com/benefits-of-national-parks/

Shebby Lee Tours: Journeys of exploration & discovery since 1978. (n.d.). Shebby Lee Tours. https://www.shebbyleetours.com/

Sights to see - Great Basin National Park. (2023, July 29). National Park Service. https://www.nps.gov/grba/planyourvisit/sights-to-see.htm

Skyland on Skyline Drive. (n.d.). Shenandoah National Park. https://www.goshenandoah.com/lodging/skyland

Southern Hills Region. (n.d.). Back Hills & Badlands. https://www.blackhillsbadlands.com/region/southern-hills

Spotting wildlife in the Badlands. (2021, May 11). National Park Service. https://www.nps.gov/thingstodo/badl-wildlife-viewing.htm

Starr, M. (2022, March 1). *8 spectacular wineries near Shenandoah National Park (+ map).* Virginia Travel Tips. https://virginiatraveltips.com/wineries-near-shenandoah-national-park/

Stehekin Pastry Company. (n.d.). TripAdvisor. https://www.tripadvisor.

com/Restaurant_Review-g58765-d2317353-Reviews-Stehekin_
Pastry_Company-Stehekin_Washington.html

Stehekin Valley Ranch. (n.d.). Stehekin Valley Ranch. https://
stehekinvalleyranch.com/

Sun Mountain Lodge. (n.d.). TripAdvisor. https://www.tripadvisor.com/
Hotel_Review-g58833-d114307-Reviews-Sun_Mountain_
Lodge-Winthrop_Washington.html

T Pattenn Cafe. (n.d.). TripAdvisor. https://www.tripadvisor.com/
Restaurant_Review-g43399-d3739386-Reviews-T_Pattenn_
Cafe-Orr_Minnesota.html

The 12 best street markets in Badlands National Park. (2023, July 16).
Wanderlog. https://wanderlog.com/list/geoCategory/174079/
best-street-markets-in-badlands-national-park#hours

The best 10 grocery near North Cascades Lodge at Stehekin in Stehekin, WA.
(n.d.). Yelp. https://www.yelp.com/search?cflt=grocery&find_
near=north-cascades-lodge-at-stehekin-stehekin

The best 10 shopping near MN, MN. (n.d.). Yelp. https://
www.yelp.com/search?cflt=shopping&find_

Made in the USA
Coppell, TX
06 July 2024

34305688R00098